The Girls' Guide to Losing Your -Plates

The Girls' Guide to Losing Your L-Plates

How to Pass Your Driving Test

MARIA McCARTHY

SIMON &
SCHUSTER

London · New York · Sydney · Toronto

A CBS COMPANY

First published by Pocket Books, 2007
An imprint of Simon & Schuster UK Ltd
This edition published by Simon & Schuster UK Ltd, 2011
A CBS COMPANY

1 3 5 7 9 10 8 6 4 2

Simon & Schuster UK Ltd
1st floor
222 Gray's Inn Road
London
WC1X 8HB

www.simonandschuster.co.uk

Simon & Schuster Australia
Sydney

A CIP catalogue record for this book is
available from the British Library.

Illustrations by Kat Heyes

ISBN: 978-1-89983-560-2

Typeset by Rowland Phototypesetting Ltd,
Bury St Edmunds, Suffolk
Printed in the UK by Cox & Wyman, Reading, Berkshire RG1 8EX

For my parents,
John and Kate McCarthy

Contents

Acknowledgements

I'm tremendously grateful to everyone who has helped during the research and writing of *The Girls' Guide to Losing Your L-Plates*.

I'm indebted to Dr Peter Russell, Professor of Road Safety at the Driver Education Research Foundation; Eddie Barnaville of the Driving Instructors Association; Neil Greig, Head of Policy at the Automobile Association Motoring Trust in Scotland; Kevin Delaney of the Royal Automobile Club; Vince Yearley of the Institute of Advanced Motorists; Vicky Stone of Learn and Live; Bob Smalley of the Royal Society for Prevention of Accidents; Gladeana McMahon of the British Association for Counselling and Psychotherapy; Denise Knowles of Relate; clinical psychologist Dr Josh Carritt-Baker; hypnotherapist Diana Ballantyne; Malcolm Tarling and Lucy Butler of the Association of British Insurers; Nigel Bartran of Norwich Union and Stuart Neill of Tesco Motor Insurance.

I couldn't have written this book without help from the driving instructors who shared their expertise so generously. Many thanks to Chris Pope, Clive Greenaway, Malcolm Fortnam, Tony Friday, Liz Mitchell, Charlie Walmesley, Peter Blackburn and Christopher Marquis of the AA. I'm especially grateful to driving consultant Kathy Higgins whose detailed feedback and advice was much appreciated – I'm so glad I found you!

Amanda Preston has been a fantastic agent, wise and supportive from the very beginning – many thanks to her and everyone else at Luigi Bonomi Associates. And I still can't believe my luck in having such a wonderfully talented and perceptive editor as Edwina Barstow – I've valued her sound judgement more than I can say.

A huge thank you is due to the friends who shared their experiences of learning to drive with such honesty and humour – Philippa, Rebecca, Juliette, Anna, Kate, Sandra, Imogen, Helen, Ruby, Liz, Shelley, Rosy, Julia, Margaret, Jane, Laura, Lynne, Jenny, Ellen, Elaine and Matthew.

Finally, I'd like to give very special thanks to Charlie for succeeding where others had failed and getting me through my own driving test and to Stuart, for whose kindness and patience on our practice drives I will be forever grateful.

Do check out my website for useful driving links and more learner-driver experiences. I'd also appreciate any feedback on the book. www.mariamccarthy.co.uk

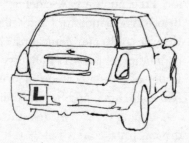

Chapter 1

Getting into Gear

Being able to drive is a wonderful thing, bringing fun, freedom and independence. Actually passing your driving test on the other hand can be a daunting business. A talented few breeze through after a handful of lessons with an instructor and a bit of practice with their partner or parents. But most of us aren't that lucky. For most of us, it costs money we'd rather be spending on clothes and time we'd rather be spending with mates or having a lie-in. And that's even before you get to the humiliation of feeling that you'll never be able to manage a successful parallel park or the sweaty-palmed, stomach-churning horrors of driving-test nerves.

This is where *The Girls' Guide to Losing Your L-Plates* comes in. It will provide information, support and encouragement and, among other things:

- Help you find the right driving instructor (and get rid of the wrong one such as the Gossip, the Short-Changer or the Lech!).
- Show you how to get the most out of your lessons – how finding out the local test centre routes, using visualization techniques and wearing the right shoes can all help your progress.
- Tell you how to survive the humiliation of crying in front of your driving instructor.
- Offer advice on how to have driving practice with your partner and remain on speaking terms.
- Provide vital tips for overcoming driving-test nerves.
- Help you believe that you *can* get there, even after a

disastrous lesson or when you've just failed your test for the fifth time.

- Discover if there's any truth behind those driving-test myths such as 'You've got to set your rear-view mirror slightly off so it's really obvious that you're looking into it', 'Driving examiners have a quota to pass every week, so it's down to luck, really', or 'If you wear a short skirt a male examiner will be too busy drooling to notice if you make a mistake.'

The book also provides useful facts and figures on learning to drive and entertaining snippets of driving trivia. There are ex-learners' accounts of the agony and ecstasy of gaining their licence – and how it's all been worth it for the freedom and independence that driving brings. It isn't intended to cover the technical side of learning to drive, that's for a qualified driving instructor. And it isn't about encouraging you to have the minimum number of lessons to scrape through your test at the earliest opportunity. Your aim should be to become a safe and confident driver for life and so it's vital that you can consistently drive to a high standard before taking your test.

History of the driving test

1893 – France was the first country in the world to introduce a driving test, along with vehicle registration plates and parking restrictions.

1900 – Vera Hedges Butler was the first British woman to pass a driving test. As they hadn't yet started in

Britain the keen-as-mustard Miss Hedges Butler went all the way to Paris to take the French test.

June 1935 – Driving tests began in the UK. They cost 37^1/2p (7s/6d) and the pass rate was 63 per cent. The first person to pass was called Mr Beene (yes, really). There weren't any test centres and examiners would meet candidates at a pre-arranged spot like a park or railway station.

September 1939 – Driving tests were suspended for the duration of World War II and resumed on 1 November 1946.

November 1956–April 1957 – Testing was suspended again during the Suez Crisis.

May 1975 – Demonstrating arm signals is no longer required.

April 1991 – A bleak date for those of us who struggle with going backwards as a reverse parking manoeuvre becomes a compulsory part of the test.

July 1996 – A separate theory test is introduced. Before this the driving examiner would ask some Highway Code questions at the end of the test.

November 2002 – The theory test is expanded to include the hazard perception test.

September 2003 – The Show me/Tell me vehicle safety questions are added to the beginning of the practical test.

Present day – The Driving Standards Agency (DSA) now conducts 1.5 million car tests and 1.5 million theory tests a year. Thirty-two million people in the UK currently hold driving licences – 70 per cent of the adult population (National Travel Survey, Department for Transport (DfT) 2004).

Despite the time, expense and emotional trauma they cause, driving tests are undeniably a Very Good Thing because they make our roads safer. In 1934 there were only 2.5 million vehicles on Britain's roads but 7,343 people were killed in road accidents. However, by 2004 there were over 30 million vehicles on the road and the Department of Transport report on road casualties (2004) quoted 3,221 fatalities.

Your road to success

Your first step to becoming a driver is to get your provisional driving licence. The minimum age for holding one is seventeen, unless you are in receipt of the higher rate of Disability Living Allowance, in which case the age is sixteen. You can apply for your provisional licence two months in advance of your seventeenth birthday. You'll need to get the relevant form from a post office, complete all relevant sections and send it off to the Driver and Vehicle Licensing Agency (DVLA) Swansea. The full address is shown on the application form. When you're signing it, make sure your signature fits inside the box, rather than scrawled all over the place. This signature is transferred to your licence, so all of it needs to be within the assigned space. You also need to include a passport-sized photo, which then ends up on your full licence – so make sure it's a decent one! The licence can take several weeks to arrive, longer if your medical history needs to be checked by the DVLA. Your driving instructor will need to inspect both the photocard and paper parts of your provisional licence at the start of your first lesson. If you don't have your licence then it's illegal for them to take you out.

Next, to get a full driving licence, you'll need to pass the theory and practical tests, which are covered in detail in later chapters. All you have to do to get the provisional licence is take a trip to the post office, which shouldn't be too difficult. However, passing the theory and, in particular, the practical test will take hard work and probably involve some ups and downs, which is why it's vital to have both the confidence to know that you're capable of getting your driving licence and the commitment to keep going through any difficult patches.

Believe in yourself

When you're driving round a housing estate at 20 m.p.h. but still managing to stall the car and reverse into bollards, it's difficult to believe that you'll ever make that magical transformation into the confident, breezy sort of girl who can deal capably with heavy city traffic, or bomb along a busy motorway. However, what you need to remember is that everyone was a beginner once and many people will have shared the doubts and fears that you're having now, but most have gone on to become safe and confident drivers – and so can you.

Keeping your motivation strong

'To achieve a challenging goal you've got to be willing to break it down into a number of parts and tackle each stage in turn,' says Gladeana McMahon, psychologist and spokesperson for the British Association for Counselling and Psychotherapy. 'Don't give yourself a hard time about not being able to do everything perfectly straight away. Motivation is vital so keep yours strong by making a list of why you really want to learn to drive and of the things you'll enjoy doing once you've passed your test – then if you hit a bad patch you can refer to it and it'll keep you focused.' For example:

- I can get to work without the journey taking one and a half hours and two changes of train.
- I can visit my boyfriend in Sheffield without being crammed on to a horrible crowded coach for four hours.
- Late at night I'll feel safer in my car than using public transport.
- I won't have to haul the supermarket shopping around on the bus.
- It'll be much easier to take my baby out and about.
- I'll be able to follow my chosen career.
- I'll be able to get into the car on impulse and go anywhere I like – to the sea, to visit friends, to festivals.
- I won't have to sit on the bus being driven insane by other people's novelty ringtones.

Another helpful motivational tip is to cut out a picture of your dream car and stick it on your noticeboard or fridge – every time you look at it, imagine yourself sitting confidently behind that wheel.

Overcoming your doubts and fears

If there's anything about the prospect of learning to drive that's bothering you, it's far better to admit it to yourself than sweep it under the carpet. Facing up to your anxieties then allows you to come up with practical strategies to overcome them.

Gladeana McMahon suggests a useful technique for dealing with any worries. 'On one side of a piece of paper, write down all your fears – no matter how trivial or silly they may seem. Then on the other side write down positive statements to counter them. That'll help you see that with commitment and a positive attitude you will be able to achieve your goal.' For example:

Clutch, gears, getting into lane, watching out for other traffic – it's all too much to take in!
I don't have to learn everything at once. My instructor will break down every step into manageable stages and then putting it all together will be a breeze.

I go to pieces in exams and the thought of someone watching my every move freaks me out!
There are loads of good techniques for handling nerves – using them will help me stay calm and show how well I can drive.

My sister and friends have all learnt really quickly. What if I take ages and they make fun of me?
So what? People learn different things at different rates and there are plenty of things I'm better at than them.

I'm too old.
Learning new things is possible at any age – and tackling new challenges will help keep my mind sharp.

L

Remind yourself of your past achievements

Another useful strategy is to make a list of your past achievements. Some of them will be things that you thought you'd find really difficult, or could never manage – but you did them anyway. For example:

- I passed my GCSE Chemistry despite failing it in my mocks.
- I got over splitting up with Tom/Dick/Harry.
- I made new friends after moving schools.
- I've given birth!
- I dropped a dress size last summer.
- I'm a good cook.

Now all you've got to do is add 'I passed my driving test' to that list!

Giving yourself a head start

Here are some ways you could get started on learning to drive even before you get your provisional licence.

- When you're a passenger in a car or bus start watching the way the traffic flows into different lanes, the judgements that are made about when to pull out at roundabouts or junctions.
- Ask family and friends to explain different manoeuvres to you, ideally when they're carrying them out in the

car – though miming them at home can work quite well too.

- Start revising for your theory test by checking out road signs as you travel.
- If you have any doubts at all about your eyesight, get it checked out before your first lesson. Your instructor will probably test you on reading a number plate at a distance of twenty metres before you set off and if you fail he'll refuse to take you out.
- Some driving schools offer off-road tuition for 16-year-olds so if you're eager to get started this would be a good way to get some practice under your belt. However, beware of driving schools that teach 'off-road' in supermarket car parks or other private land that is open to public use – their car insurance is invalid there and it's a sign that their approach is going to be unprofessional in other ways as well. The only place you can legally teach drivers before they receive their provisional licence is private land that's gated off from the public (which is why farmers' children tend to learn so early!) and designated venues such as driving centres.

I was desperate to pass my test as soon as I could so I started to watch the way my parents handled roundabouts or heavy traffic and ask them questions about parking – by the time I started my lessons I already felt I knew loads. Hannah, 18

Money, money, money

Learning to drive can be an expensive business. And there are few things more frustrating than getting almost to the point of passing your test and then having to stop because you've run out of money. So it's important to have the finances sorted out beforehand and either have the cash available or an idea of how you're going to raise it as you go along. Here are a few facts and figures to give you an idea of the sort of bill you could be looking at:

Provisional licence and test fees

Provisional licence: £50*
Theory test: £31
Practical test: £62 (weekdays), £75 (evenings and weekends)
Total (assuming that you pass the theory and practical tests
    first time): £143 (£156)

However, the average number of practical tests women take to pass is 2.12, so be prepared to budget for additional tests if necessary.

Lesson costs

When comparing the cost of lessons from different schools, it's important to find out what period of time you get for your money. Some lessons that are quoted as being very cheap are actually only forty-five minutes. However, standard lesson length tends to be an hour. Obviously, how many lessons it takes to pass is going to vary hugely between individuals. It'll depend a lot on your natural driving ability. Driving is one of those skills that some people pick up easily but others struggle

* All figures were correct at the time of going to press.

with. The strugglers can go on to become perfectly safe and confident drivers; it's just that getting there is more expensive. However, driving lessons aren't a suitable area for cost-cutting. Don't pick the cheapest teacher you can get, go for the one you think is best. After all, you're learning a skill that you'll be using for the rest of your life – and getting the right instructor could turn out to be less expensive in the long run anyway.

When I was researching driving instructors I spoke to one who I had a really good vibe about – he was clearly enthusiastic about teaching and very understanding about how nervous I was. But he was more expensive than most instructors so I went with another one who turned out to be rubbish at explaining things. After two failed tests I changed to an instructor who was a bit better, and eventually scraped through on my fifth attempt. In retrospect, I feel I should have trusted my instincts and gone with the instructor I thought was best in the first place – I'm sure I'd have learnt much faster and saved money in the long run too.
Naomi, 34

The DfT commissioned a sample group study of learner drivers in 2004 that showed that women, on average, had taken 51.9 lessons from a qualified driving instructor before passing (the figure for men was 36.2). Chris Marquis, Training Manager of the Automobile Association (AA) Driving School, suggests that for a ballpark figure you take your age then double it to calculate the number of lessons you'll need. Calculating the projected cost from the national average for women – fifty-two lessons at £24 a lesson comes to £1248. Calculating the projected cost using Chris's age-linked formula, a 17-year-old would need thirty-four lessons and at £24 each this would cost £816. A 30-year-old would need sixty lessons and at £24 each this would cost £1440.

Most people are surprised by these figures, as many of their family and friends will have reported learning in far fewer lessons – maybe between ten and twenty. But like number of sexual partners, how many driving lessons people take is a figure that's often adjusted downwards! Chris Marquis says that 'There's a standing joke among driving instructors that if you ask someone how many lessons they took to pass they'll divide the number by two and subtract ten.' And then, of course, the average is bumped up by those of us who take lots and lots of lessons to succeed. But whether you anticipate taking just a few lessons or needing lots, it's important to plan carefully for the possible cost of learning to drive – and then if you do learn quickly you'll have even more to spend on your first car!

Some tips for keeping the cost down

- Some driving schools offer discounts on block bookings or to pay for your theory and practical test fees. However, when it comes to block bookings it's a good idea to have at least one lesson with them first, otherwise you could find yourself committed to a series of lessons with an instructor you don't click with.
- Lesson fees at the larger schools such as the AA vary depending on location. For example, a one-hour lesson in central London currently costs £26.25, whereas one in Walthamstow costs £23.25. So if you commute into central London and are considering whether to have lessons from work or home, this could be a deciding factor.
- There are driving schools which offer discounts for students, single parents or unemployed people.
- You could ask friends and relatives to give you driving-lesson vouchers or payment towards them as gifts for birthdays or Christmas.

- Getting lots of practice outside of lessons will help you become more confident behind the wheel.
- Learn to handle your driving-test nerves effectively. To have been told by your driving instructor that you've reached the right standard but to fail because of nerves and have to shell out more cash for lessons and test fees is incredibly frustrating. So the right techniques for over-coming nervousness (as described in Chapter 7) can save you hundreds of pounds.

Paying for my driving lessons was pure torture. I took lessons in the uni holidays when I was living at home and working at two different café jobs to earn some money. I failed twice and had to have more lessons and pay for more tests. As I was on the minimum wage it took hours of wiping down tables and loading the dishwasher to pay for a single driving lesson but I wouldn't give up. It was all worth it in the end as I got offered my dream job in PR just after graduating and I wouldn't have had a chance if I hadn't had my licence! Imogen, 22

Hopefully learning to drive won't cost you as much as it did Venida Crabtree, a 50-year-old masseuse from Cowley, Oxfordshire. Venida started taking lessons in 1972 and went on to spend £27,000 on 2000 lessons and failed 104 times before finally passing her driving test in July 2005!

Chapter 2

Decisions, Decisions

You've got your provisional licence and you've budgeted for your lessons, now it's time to find the right instructor. When it comes to learning to drive, this is one of the most important decisions you'll make. Getting the best person for you will make the process more enjoyable, quicker and have long-term benefits for your future as a driver. So choose carefully and don't settle for second best.

Finding the best driving school and instructor for you

Personal recommendation

Most people agree that the best way to find a good driving instructor is through personal recommendation and often that can work really well. But although it can be helpful, personal recommendation isn't the Holy Grail. Teaching is a very individual thing and the instructor who was ideal for your best mate, who's been helping his dad tinker with cars for years, isn't necessarily going to be suited to you if you're the type who's still getting the indicators and the windscreen wipers muddled up on your sixth lesson. If you try him and give up in despair you might then move on to your second recommendation – the 'wonderful, patient man' who taught your Auntie

Sue six years ago – but when you call him up it turns out he's retired. Which leaves only the instructor who taught your flatmate and tut-tutted and rolled his eyes so much that she regularly came home in tears and only passed on her fourth attempt.

Getting one out of the phone book or via the internet

Hmm . . . so maybe it would be better to try the phone book. You open it up and there are the driving schools – dozens of them. Big ones, small ones, ones offering intensive courses, female instructors, special payment deals. The internet can also be a useful source for finding driving schools – Google 'driving school' plus your area and see what comes up. You can also check out the websites of the large driving schools such as the AA. Rather than sticking in a pin, choosing the cheapest or one where the name ('Jude's School of Motoring' 'Orlando-Drive') catches your eye for some reason, it's worth thinking carefully about what would suit you best. Here are some points you might like to consider:

Availability – Do you want a school that offers lessons during evenings and weekends or before work?

Lesson duration – If you possibly can, it's a good idea to have two-hour lessons rather than go for one hour. You're able to settle into your driving more and can go further afield to experience different situations such as city or country roads.

Location, location, location – Where should your driving school be based? Would it be more convenient for you to be picked up from your home or your work/school/college – or both? If you live out in the sticks but the test routes are in the town where you work, it would be worth considering having lessons from there, so you don't have a lengthy (and expensive) journey in before you even practise the test routes.

A large or small school? – The larger schools such as the AA have got a pool of instructors so if your own is unavailable because of holidays or illness you'll be offered a replacement without having to have a break in your lessons. However, this can be a mixed blessing as instructors often have their own teaching styles and having someone new can affect the continuity of your lessons. Small schools also offer a personal approach and the successful ones tend to get most of their business from recommendations from satisfied ex-pupils. They can sometimes be cheaper than the major driving schools.

A male or female instructor? – At the moment only 15 per cent of the 30,000 driving instructors on the DSA register are female, and the good ones are very much in demand. Some women much prefer to be taught by another woman – maybe because they prefer female company, because they've had problems in the past with lecherous instructors, or because they feel a woman would be more sensitive and sympathetic. In fact, there are sympathetic male instructors and female ones who are critical, so this is something that it's best to judge on the individual's personality rather than their gender.

Manual or automatic car? – Most people choose to learn in a manual car. This means you gain a full driving licence and can then go on to drive a manual or automatic car in the future. If, however, you pass your test in an automatic that's the only sort of car you're then qualified to drive. If you want to drive a manual car you'll have to retake your test in one. If you think you might want to hire cars in the future, bear in mind that this is easier if you have a manual licence as there aren't as many automatic cars available.

The advantage of learning in a manual is the flexibility, but if you've had problems learning to drive in the past, or if you're seriously daunted by the prospect, you might want to consider an automatic. 'Because you don't have to learn to use the clutch and gears, it's a much simpler process and means you can give more of your attention to what's happening on the road,' says driving instructor Charlie Walmesley. 'I've seen people who were really struggling have their relationship with driving completely transformed.'

Assistance with the theory test – Most driving instructors will offer help with the theory test in the sense of asking you about the Highway Code, or testing you with sample questions. They'll also answer any questions you might have. If you feel you may have problems with the theory test you might want to choose a driving school that can offer you extra support.

Make and model of car – Would you like to learn in the sort of car that you might buy in the future? There are schools offering Nissans, Vauxhalls, Fords, Peugeots and Minis, so if you are dithering between a few choices you could let your preferred car be the deciding factor.

If you have a disability – Some driving schools offer specialized tuition for drivers with disabilities – such as modified cars, or instructors who have learnt sign language to assist deaf students. (See the reference section for details of organizations that can point you in the right direction.)

If you're pregnant – 'Pregnant women aren't invalids and if you feel well there's no reason you shouldn't learn to drive when you're expecting a baby,' says Bob Smalley, Chief Driving Examiner for Advanced Drivers and Riders at the Royal Society for Prevention of Accidents (RoSPA).

It's important to wear your seat belt the correct way as your pregnancy progresses – that is, with the lower strap under the bump. Your instructor will give you advice on this. During the later stages of pregnancy it can feel difficult to twist around in your seat to do the reversing manoeuvres – but again, this is something you and your instructor can work round.

However, it's important to be aware that you will have to learn the emergency stop manoeuvre and there's a one-in-three chance you'll be asked to perform it on your test. The test has to be carried out under the same conditions for everyone and it won't be possible for the examiner to make allowances for your pregnancy. If you have concerns about this, discuss them with your doctor and midwife.

Many mums-to-be learn to drive 'against the clock' as they can't face the thought of hauling their baby and the accompanying paraphernalia round on public transport. However, if your due date approaches but you're still a long way off test standard, don't let it stress you out or prompt you to push for an early test. It might be inconvenient, but you can always start your lessons again after your baby arrives. That way, you'll be able to go in for your test when you're properly prepared and be confident that you'll be safe behind the wheel.

An intensive course? – The idea of taking one of those 'first lesson Monday, test on Friday' intensive courses advertised by some driving schools can seem to offer an appealing shortcut which avoids fitting in lessons around work or college over several months. However, there are serious drawbacks that need to be considered.

'One of the problems with intensive courses is you don't have the opportunity to drive in all conditions with guidance from an instructor,' says Dr Peter Russell, Professor of Road Safety at the Driver Education Research Foundation. 'For example, if you learn to drive in the summer you might never drive in the dark during your lessons. Or if you learn in the winter you might not experience the problems of driving with the bright sun shining in your eyes.' Driving consultant Kathy Higgins agrees and adds, 'Intensive lessons leading to a test at the end of the week create a feeling of stress and pressure during the lessons – and these emotions can continue to be associated with driving long after the student has passed their test.' And it's another thumbs-down from driving instructor Liz Mitchell, 'If you have a bad lesson you can't just put it behind you and try again another day – you just have to keep flogging away at it.' Chris Marquis of the AA also has reservations about complete beginners taking week-long intensive courses. 'It's a tremendous amount to assimilate in such a short period of time,' he says. 'It can have a short, sharp push value for people with some experience in the past – for example, if you've had lessons but failed your test and want to get going again. If you want to make progress fast then I feel that taking two-hour lessons every day is acceptable but more than that can be self-defeating.'

Smoking – The vast majority of instructors wouldn't smoke in their cars. But if you dislike the smell of cigarette smoke, it's worth finding out if a potential instructor smokes at all, as you might not like the smell in their car. If, on the other hand, you'd find it really hard to get through a two-hour lesson without a smoking break, you might want to find an instructor who is sympathetic to that.

Length of lessons – As mentioned in the previous chapter, when you're enquiring about lessons, check how long they are. The reason why some lessons seem so much cheaper than others is because you're being quoted for forty-five minutes, rather than an hour.

Added extras – Some driving schools offer added extras such as a system whereby your lesson is videoed and you can play it back in your spare time and learn from watching what you did. If the prospect of this or other added extras appeals to you get in touch with the schools that offer them and find out more.

Post-test support/Pass Plus support – Many driving schools offer the option of having a motorway lesson after you've passed your test. Some are registered to teach the Pass Plus course. This is a training course for new drivers specially designed by the DSA which involves tuition over a wide range of road and traffic situations. Taking the course can make you a safer driver and save on car insurance as well. (For more details see Chapter 9: 'You've Passed: Losing Your L-Plates' and call Pass Plus or check out their website.) If you know you're going to want to take this course and would prefer to stick with the same instructor, then it's a good idea to choose one who's registered to teach it.

Doing your research

Hopefully, considering the above points should have narrowed things down and given you a list of potential driving schools. The next thing to do is to phone them up and have an initial chat. First, it's important to check that you'd be taught by a fully qualified Approved Driving Instructor (ADI), who must have passed a three-part examination run by the DSA and have their name entered on their register. They must display a green octagonal ADI certificate on their car windscreen (a pink triangle one means the instructor is a trainee). Some driving schools use trainee instructors to give lessons – but it's best to avoid these and find a fully qualified instructor. Ask what standard of instructor you'll be taught by when you call, and double-check their badge when they turn up. It's also important that they're fully insured. For peace of mind it's best to choose an instructor who's a member of the Driving Instructors Association (DIA). This ensures they have public liability cover of £5,000,000. Look out for the DIA badge in their advertisements or on their training car.

The standard of teaching of ADIs is regularly checked by the DSA through a supervisor sitting in on a live lesson. The instructor is then graded: grade 4 is competent; grade 5 is good; grade 6 is a very high standard. It's a good idea to ask a potential instructor for their grade before embarking on a course of lessons. But just as important is the 'feel' you get from them. In their adverts, many driving schools claim to provide 'fun, friendly and patient tuition'. But then it's not exactly in their interests to admit to being boring and grumpy, is it? A chat over the phone followed by a trial lesson is the best way to assess if this is the right person for you – and be willing to trust your gut instinct and look for another instructor if you feel unsure about them. As Dr Peter Russell, Professor of Road Safety, says, 'A grading is a "snapshot" of how an instructor performs on a particular lesson on a particular day, when they're being inspected. And although grading is a significant factor to consider, it's also important that you feel safe, confident and relaxed with your instructor. When there's a sense of rapport between instructor and pupil, learning is so much easier.'

Driving instructors to avoid

The Gossip – His golf handicap, his divorce, his holiday. This driving instructor wants to talk about everything except your driving and will continue to ramble on even when you're sweating over a manoeuvre and are in serious need of some help and advice. A certain amount of social chat can be fine and even relaxing. But if you feel he's not giving you enough attention this needs to be dealt with – you're paying for his time after all. Rather than putting up with it explain that you find too much chatting distracting and you'd rather you both just concentrated on the driving. Hopefully, that should sort the problem out. If not, it's time to look for another instructor.

The Critic – By their very nature driving instructors have to give feedback, but it should be aimed at helping you to do better rather than bringing you down. This is a very personal thing and an instructor whose blunt approach is appreciated by one student could be found really scary by a less confident one. If your instructor's criticism is bringing you down, tell him you feel you could do with more encouragement. If he doesn't take your comments on board then it's probably time to change.

The Short-changer – As we all know, traffic can be unpredictable, so it's understandable if your instructor occasionally turns up late. However, this time should be made up to ensure you've got the full hour you've paid for – if not straight away then at a later lesson. A few instructors can sometimes take advantage by 'just popping into' a shop or bank during your lesson time – this shouldn't happen but if it does the time should be made up. In some driving schools it's common practice for a student to take the previous one home during the first part of their lesson. However, this can be embarrassing and means you're often likely to be doing the route to their home rather than practising test ones. The whole lesson should be focused on improving your driving skills, not using you as a taxi service to ferry around other learners. This is a school to avoid.

The Lech – This is one to get rid of straight away. If you feel that your driving instructor is making over-personal remarks, trying to stare down your blouse or (shudder!) being unnecessarily tactile, then terminate your lessons and find someone else. If you are upset by his behaviour then you should report it to the DSA.

Some ex-learners on their driving instructors

The good guys and girls

There are loads of good driving instructors out there – patient, capable, supportive, inspiring and basically great teachers! When the instructor and learner 'gel' lessons are far more relaxed and you absorb those vital skills so much more effectively. Get a driving instructor who you feel like this about and you're well on the way to passing!

> *My first instructor was a disaster but my second had a way of making me feel that my mistakes were minor glitches and overall I was making progress, which made all the difference to my confidence. I stopped finding my lessons a humiliating ordeal and became far more receptive to learning.* Siobhan, 29

> *I'm quite an emotional person but Sue stayed calm no matter how stressed out I got. She stuck with me through three tests, all of which I failed disastrously through nerves. She's got the patience of a saint and I'm not sure I could have done it without her.* Rachel, 40

And the ones who could do better (or who should give up entirely)!

> *My first driving instructor used to get stoned and spent our lessons ogling girls behind his sunglasses and not bothering to talk to me.* Eva, 33

> *My first driving instructor was really old and so quiet during our lessons I sometimes used to worry that he'd died or something. He hardly spoke, just used to make these vague hand gestures and I was meant to work out from them whether I should go left or right. I stuck with him for ages before changing but it was money down the drain! Then I tried a woman instructor because I thought she'd be more sympathetic but she wasn't. She was very smartly dressed with perfect hair and nails and I felt she looked down on me for being a bit hippyish and having piercings. When I did anything wrong she'd tut-tut until I just wanted to crawl under the seat. To be fair though, she did get me through my test.* Janine, 18

If it takes several trial lessons before you find an instructor who feels right for you, then so be it. After all, if you were shopping for shoes you wouldn't buy the first pair you tried on. Remember that it's your money and you'll be paying rather a lot of it to the instructor you choose, so it's important to get the right one. And once your lessons have started it's important to make the most of every minute of them (especially since – to take an average – a minute equals 40p!). The next chapter will give you tips on how to absorb this new skill as quickly and thoroughly as possible, and how to keep up your spirits during the lessons that really don't go your way.

Chapter 3

Making the Most of Your Lessons

And you're off! You've booked your lessons and you're sitting beside your instructor. Not only that, but you're actually in the driving seat, surrounded by pedals, brakes and gear levers which one day you'll have mastered. You could be feeling terrified, excited, impatient to get going – or a bewildering cocktail of all these emotions.

I felt very daunted as I hadn't been a cyclist, had no road-sense and no confidence in my ability to control a car. My impression was that cars were powerful things with minds of their own, liable to leap forward or jolt to a stop and make loud noises and that I would never be able to drive one. Abigail, 27

I grew up in the middle of nowhere and was desperate to pass my test as soon as possible. I used to look forward to my lessons, because I felt that even the difficult ones were taking me towards my goal of becoming independent. Laura, 17

Some learners have a natural aptitude for driving, relate well to their instructor and find the process exciting and enjoyable – hopefully you're going to be one of them. However, many of us have times when we hit rough patches. When that happens it's easy to feel as though you're the only person ever to have struggled or worried that you're never going to make it.

This chapter is aimed at showing you you're not alone. Whether it's dreading your lessons, feeling that you'll never master a particular manoeuvre or crying in front of your instructor, there are plenty of ex-learners out there who've been through identical traumas and have gone on to become confident and skilful drivers. It will also provide guidance on understanding the learning process and making the most of your lessons from the very first time that you sit behind the wheel till the final polishing up of your skills before your test.

Before setting off

What not to wear

Like most things in life, driving is easier if you're wearing the right outfit. Fortunately, in this instance, you're not going to have to spend next month's wages on designer clobber – any comfortable clothes will do. However, the right footwear is vital. Heels are best avoided as it's difficult to get the leverage you'll need to operate the pedals. And boots or trainers with thick soles aren't a good idea either as they make it difficult to feel the clutch bite. Trainers with thinner soles are fine though. Avoid flip-flops because they can slide off too easily. And don't drive without shoes. Who do you think you are, Joss Stone?

Medicines

Before taking any medication, check the label to make sure it doesn't affect your ability to drive. For example, some hay fever and cold remedies can promote drowsiness, as can certain antidepressants. If you're using an over-the-counter remedy then consult the pharmacist for the right option and in the case of prescribed medication talk to your doctor.

Your first few lessons

These will probably be spent in quiet locations getting to grips with the car. 'There are two aspects to driving,' explains driving instructor Clive Greenaway. 'Car control and road-craft, and they're completely different things. Car control is learning how to handle the car itself – stopping, starting, parking and so on. Roadcraft is dealing with everything that's happening on the road – such as other vehicles, roundabouts and hazards. If a pupil takes sixty lessons, then eight to ten will probably involve learning about car control and the other fifty will be roadcraft. It's very important to get on top of controlling the car before you hit the heavy traffic, otherwise the student has too much information to process at once.'

Car control is a lot to take in initially. It's a physical process which requires a new range of conditioned reflexes, response times and hand-to-eye co-ordination skills. Even a simple procedure like moving off involves dealing with the clutch, gears, handbrake, indicators and checking the mirrors – it's like you're in multitasking overdrive. It might feel difficult to believe at the moment, but this will get easier. Eventually you'll be carrying out the correct sequence automatically. It's a bit like learning how to tie your shoelaces – your first attempts will have been a real effort, involving much concentration and guidance from your mum, but now it's something you do without a second thought.

The first steps of learning a skill are the most difficult because you're still at the stage where you have to remember everything – the knowledge is in the conscious part of your brain. However, the more it is absorbed the more it becomes subconscious and automatic, and the space freed up in your conscious mind allows you to pay greater attention to what's going on around you on the roads.

You might discover that as you progress to driving in heavier traffic, you find yourself getting flustered and feeling that you're holding everyone up when other cars are behind you, waiting for you to pull out at a junction or complete a manoeuvre. But don't let it get to you. 'People often tend to think they're making more mistakes than other people when they're not,' says driving instructor Peter Blackburn. 'They also worry that the licensed drivers are looking down on them, but on the whole other drivers are fine. They remember that they were in your position once and will cut you some slack.'

Just the two of us

Many learners find they feel really self-conscious during their lessons and loathe the sensation of being watched by their instructor all the time. This is perfectly natural and is partly down to the fact that being tutored in a one-to-one situation can be unfamiliar. Most of us are more used to being taught in classrooms where there's the opportunity to blend into the background and to try to figure problems out for yourself if you prefer. Bob Smalley of RoSPA sympathizes. 'If you were going to choose an ideal learning environment, it certainly wouldn't be the seats in the front of a car. On the one hand, it's a claustrophobic situation and the learner can feel that their space is being invaded. If things are going badly, you can't escape from each other. But when you're driving the instructor and pupil can't make eye contact because the focus needs to be on the road, and that can make the experience seem impersonal as well.' The worst of both worlds basically! But don't worry if this makes you uncomfortable; hopefully you'll relax as you become familiar with the situation.

Get the timing right

Schedule your lessons for when you're at your most fresh and receptive to learning. Mornings are best for many people. There's a Chinese proverb which says 'an hour of instruction before noon is worth two hours after it'. Though obviously disregard this advice if you don't fully wake up till lunchtime.

Start preparing for your theory test

It's a good idea to start preparing for your theory test from your first few lessons. When you're driving along it can feel as though there's a tremendous amount to take in and understanding the road signs and markings will help you feel more on top of things.

Pin up a map of your test centre area

This is particularly useful if you've got a rubbish sense of direction. If you're accustomed to familiar bus routes or walking everywhere, then whizzing round bypasses and suddenly finding yourself in a different part of town thinking, 'How on earth did I get here?' can leave you feeling very out of control. Studying a map of the relevant area can help you become more aware of what's going on. You can also mark difficult areas on it – such as sneaky one-way streets or double mini-roundabouts – so you can psyche yourself up for them as you approach rather than feel that they're coming at you out of nowhere! You might also want to mark the test routes on your map. These are available on the DSA website – type in the name of your test centre and you can download them from there. Most centres have between sixteen and twenty-two routes, with the exception of very rural places such as the Isle of Skye (Portree), which has three. The routes are designed to be equal in terms of difficulty – a mixture of easy and more challenging junctions, right and left crossings and so on. However, don't let knowing them allow you to become complacent. Driving examiners can change the route in response to roadworks or traffic jams and take you off in a completely unexpected direction.

Invest in some learning aids

The DSA produces a CD-ROM showing a test in action, and some companies have developed DVDs and CD-ROMs which give tutorial sessions, or let you practise driving a 3D car using the mouse. (See 'Reference Section' for details.)

Enjoy the learning process

If you're finding driving a struggle, it's tempting to deal with it by telling yourself, 'Right, I'm having my lessons, it's being taken care of' and feel that all you have to do is turn up, grit your teeth, count the minutes till the lesson is over and then scramble out of the car thinking, 'Phew, at least I won't have to do that again until next Tuesday.' But although that strategy will get you through a situation like ongoing dental work where all that's required of you is to be a passive patient, learning to drive is an active process and the more you engage with it, the easier it will be.

Studies have shown that people learn more effectively when they're happy and relaxed so you owe it to yourself to make your lessons positive experiences. How you do that is going to depend on your personal situation, but it might involve:

- Changing your driving instructor if you don't feel comfortable with them.
- If you've got a perfectionist streak and tend to beat yourself up when you don't get everything right first time, then see this as an opportunity for learning to be less hard on yourself.
- Focus on the aspects of driving you do enjoy, such as bowling along a clear bit of dual carriageway with a liberating speed limit. Tell yourself, 'I love driving, me!' If you think it often enough, you'll come to believe it.
- Recognize learning to drive as an important rite of passage and give it the respect and attention it deserves. Watching the traffic as a passenger, chatting with other learners on internet forums (see 'Reference Section' for details) or using positive visualization as described in Chapter 7 will help stop you 'closing down' around driving when the going gets tough and keep you actively learning.

Getting up to speed

'Learning is a very individual process,' says driving instructor Clive Greenaway. 'Some people get the basics very quickly then hit a plateau, while others take ages to get the basics but gain confidence quickly afterwards.' You might find that you have a run of good lessons, then hit the 'lesson from hell' when everything you've ever learnt seems to have just disappeared from your head. Or you could find that it takes more than just the first few lessons to settle down into your driving, and that co-ordinating the different aspects is an ongoing struggle.

> *In my lessons I always felt there was too much going on and that if I was concentrating on getting one thing right I was bound to be doing something else wrong.* Narinder, 20

But all these different scenarios are perfectly normal. The fact is that people learn at different speeds and in different ways. Quite apart from your natural aptitude, how your learning progresses can be influenced by all sorts of other factors, such as whether you grew up in a family without a car, whether you have been involved in a car accident, whether you see yourself as 'hopeless with mechanical things' and the attitudes your family and friends have towards driving. If you're concerned about money and are wondering how many lessons learning to drive might take, it can be a good idea to ask your instructor to give you an estimate after about three lessons. By then he'll probably have worked out if you're 'a natural' or someone who's likely to have to take longer than average.

Hitting a plateau

Learners often find that after a while they hit a learning plateau. Lesson after lesson is going by without much sign of improvement. This is a perfectly normal phase, and your driving instructor will probably try a range of techniques to get you past it – maybe taking a step back and concentrating on things you can do easily, to get your spirits up.

Your personal bêtes noires

As your driving progresses, you'll probably discover that there are some aspects where you feel you're making progress and others which you really struggle with. When you're sweating away over your umpteenth unsuccessful bay park or being flummoxed by lane discipline, it's easy to look at the other drivers cruising confidently past and feel that you're the only person in the history of the world to have floundered like this. But you're not! Whatever your personal driving bête noire might be, multitudes of other people will already have been humbled by it.

I hated roundabouts – we'd be approaching one and my instructor would say 'OK, we're coming to a roundabout, what do you do?' and I'd say, 'Panic!' I couldn't understand how they worked – in particular, when you have to go into the right-hand lane and then some-how move to the left to get off the horrible roundabout and back on the normal road. I thought that left on my own, I'd just have to keep going round and round and wouldn't be able to exit until there were no other cars on the roundabout at all! Rachel, 40

I really hated emergency stops. The loud noise of the instructor banging on the dashboard scared me even though I was expecting it – it was like in a horror film where you know something's about to jump out of the shadows and it frightens you even though you know it's going to happen. I hated having to stamp down on the brake and clutch, the way the car jolted to a halt, throwing us forwards in our seats – it was really nerve-racking and left me feeling totally shaken up. Eva, 33.

But just because you're struggling with something at the moment doesn't mean that you're doomed to have problems with it for ever.

I had such problems with parking when I was learning to drive – I just couldn't get the whole going backwards thing. But now I've been driving for a few years I find I can squeeze into the tightest spots effortlessly. It was as if the skill took ages to acquire, but once I'd got the basic concept I was able to sharpen it up and now I'm really rather good at it! Abigail, 27

Crying in front of your instructor

Learning to drive can bring up a turbulent mixture of emotions: frustration, anger, shame, humiliation, embarrassment and despair to name only a few. Some people cry easily, while others take more to get going. But sometimes mounting the kerb or stalling on a roundabout once too often can be all it takes to be pushed over the edge. And suddenly you're gulping, blinking, welling up . . . until you've reached the point of no return and your eyes are leaking uncontrollably! For most of us, it's one thing to cry in front of our nearest and dearest, but to sob in front of a middle-aged bloke in a bad jumper feels excruciating. Quite apart from the blotchy face and smeared mascara issue, it seems far too intimate a thing to be doing in front of someone with whom you've got a professional relationship. And unlike at work or college, dashing off to the loo to recover isn't an option – you're stuck inside the car together!

But although it might feel mortifying, it's certainly not unusual. 'We see tears all the time, men as well as women, so don't feel embarrassed,' says Chris Marquis at the AA. 'And they can be a good thing in that they're a clear sign to the instructor that they're currently asking too much of you. If a pupil cries I always say, "I blame myself for this; I've obviously been pushing you too hard." ' Although you might want to just mop yourself up and brush off the episode as soon as possible, it's better to talk it over with your instructor and tell him what's upsetting you. If he's critical and you've been upset but hiding it, it can be a turning point for him to realize that he needs to give you more support.

I was so embarrassed by crying in front of my instructor, but in retrospect I'm glad it happened. I'd been finding our lessons really tough, but instead of telling him I was just becoming quieter and more withdrawn. I think he mistook my reserve for not caring, so he was pushing me harder. Getting upset meant he worked out what was really going on. He was far less critical and more encouraging after that and I started to make much better progress. Narinder, 20

If you think you might cry, then wear waterproof mascara and have some tissues with you. Afterwards, phoning a friend and venting will help. And remember that one day this will just be an amusing anecdote.

Should I change my driving instructor?

Although you'll have made every effort to get the ideal driving instructor from the outset, as your lessons progress you could realize that he's not right for you. Maybe the problem is something obvious such as he's overcritical, doesn't seem to be keeping a proper record of your progress, or (horrors!) is a bit gropey. Or it could simply be that you're not clicking and you've got a growing sense that you'd learn more thoroughly, enjoyably and faster with someone else. But at the same time, the prospect of changing can feel like such an upheaval. After all, your instructor is getting other people through their test, so why not you? Maybe you're being unreasonable? But it's best to go with your gut feeling. 'People get stuck in a comfort zone,' says driving consultant Kathy Higgins. 'They know they're not really getting value for money, but it's like only ever having had burgers and never steak – they just don't know what they're missing. Also, pupils can develop a misplaced sense of loyalty and get into thinking, "Oh, Steve's a great bloke, I couldn't leave him," but this is one of the reasons why many substandard instructors are able to carry on. It's important to remember that you're not looking for a friend, you're looking for the best possible tuition.' But then, how best to move on? It's like when your hairdresser goes on holiday and another stylist cuts your hair while she's away and makes you look like a goddess. Next time you want to book in with her but the prospect of walking through the salon past your old hairdresser to the new one seems really embarrassing. Changing driving instructors can feel a bit like that. One option is to take the avoidance route and phone up (or better still, get your partner, flatmate or mum to) and tell him that you've run out of money or are really busy and want to stop having lessons for a while. That can be rather unsatisfactory, however; you can then live constantly on edge in case you run into him when you're out with your new instructor and have to fight the urge to sink down into your seat to avoid his wounded and accusing stare. It's best to just bite the bullet. Take a deep breath, call him and say that you don't feel you're making progress and have decided to change instructors. Be brisk and make it clear that you're not interested in any embarrassing and lengthy analysis of the situation – play the 'this has to be a quick call as I'm just popping out' card if necessary. Then put the phone down and say, 'Yippee!' You're free of a relationship that wasn't working and can start again. Have a few trial lessons with other instructors before committing yourself – this time, you want to get it right.

Dealing with loss of confidence

If you're feeling generally down about the progress you're making in your driving lessons, it can be a great boost to start getting some practice outside of them. Take advice from your instructor on when you're ready to start and see Chapter 4, 'You're Driving Me Crazy!', for advice on how to get the most out of your sessions. There are other places you can turn to for help and encouragement such as learner-driver websites. Some of the sites are visited by qualified driving instructors who can offer advice as well. (See the 'Reference Section' for details.)

Don't be afraid to experiment either – even if it seems a bit quirky! 'One ex-student built herself a sofa-car,' says Chris Marquis at the AA. 'She jammed a couple of spoons between the cushions to be the handbrake and gear lever, lay three turkey-basters in front of her to be the pedals, used a toy steering wheel and practised the control sequences in her "car". She drove for miles in that "car" and said she felt it really helped her.'

It's often said that 'Boys learn to drive more easily than girls because they play with toy cars and girls play with prams.' So OK, try playing with some toy cars. Have a little one on your desk and practise reversing it round the corner of your mouse-mat or parallel parking it between a box of paperclips and some Post-it notes. Watching the parking manoeuvre – for example, the way the rear of the car has to swing in first and then straighten up – could give you more insight into the technicalities of how it all works.

Bach flower remedies

These thirty-eight plant and flower-based remedies were developed by Dr Edward Bach, a Harley Street doctor and homoeopath. He believed they could help alter people's emotional states. The most well known is the Rescue Remedy, a mixture of five different remedies which is used at times of particular stress (such as your driving test). However, there are other remedies which can be taken for prolonged periods to help alleviate any particular emotional traumas you might have concerning your driving; for example, chestnut bud, repeating the same problems over and over; larch, expecting to fail, lack of self-confidence; rock rose, tendency to panic. Bach flower remedies are available at most health food shops, which may also offer free leaflets to help you select the right remedy for you. They're taken by mixing in a glass or bottle of water and sipping at intervals, dropped neat on to the tongue or rubbed on to the temples and wrists.

L

Visualization and positive thinking

When you're feeling down, remind yourself of all the other things you've learnt in your life, such as cooking or cycling. Chances are you struggled with those too, to start off with. Visualization is also a powerful strategy used successfully by entertainers and sports stars. See yourself successfully carrying out difficult manoeuvres or dealing confidently with heavy traffic. This will give your subconscious mind the message that you can do these things and it will help you learn more effectively.

Hitting a bad patch – should I give up?

Most people have times when they feel like giving up learning to drive. But it's never a good idea to just throw in the towel impulsively. Instead, think through your reasons and analyse them to make sure that it's a considered decision rather than a kneejerk response to a horrible lesson. Also ask yourself whether you're giving up for a valid reason or whether you're just making excuses. Only you can decide which is which!

I've already had far more lessons than any of my friends and I'm still not anywhere near being put in for my test. Are some people just doomed never to be able to drive? And if so, how can I tell if I'm one of them?

Like any skill, from computer programming to tap-dancing, there are going to be some people who pick it up easily, and others who struggle. 'People who take to driving easily often tend to be the sort of people who play sports such as tennis and football and are good at judging spatial relationships,' says driving instructor Chris Pope. 'Having had experience of the road as a cyclist or motorcyclist is also helpful. Those with problems are often bookish types – everything has to be explained to them in detail because they don't do it by instinct, as the more mechanically inclined would. I've also noticed that people in the caring professions can have problems – they're good with people, but not with machines.'

The theory of multiple intelligences put forward by psychologist Howard Gardner in 1993 claims that there isn't just one way to be intelligent, there are seven different types. It's the more practical ones, such as spatial and bodily kinaesthetic skills, that are most useful when it comes to driving. The types of intelligence are:

1. interpersonal (social skills)
2. intrapersonal (self-awareness)
3. linguistic (reading and writing)
4. logical and mathematical
5. spatial (navigating, judging distances accurately)
6. bodily kinaesthetic (to do with movement)
7. musical

If you score highly in the forms of intelligence that happen to be academically focused, such as linguistic skills, then you'll probably have got used to thinking of yourself as 'clever' or 'the sort of person who picks things up easily'. So to find yourself in a situation where those skills don't count for diddly-squit can be humbling, to put it mildly. If learning to drive matters to you, you're going to have to accept that it'll be a slog, maybe the first one you've ever encountered. Accept it as best you can, and aim to see it as character-forming. It's a good idea to talk to your driving instructor about the situation and ask how many lessons they think you might take; that way you'll be able to decide if you're currently able to make the commitment, both mentally and financially.

My family/friends all passed really easily. I'm struggling and they keep teasing me and telling me I'll never make it.

This is a situation where you shouldn't back down. Some people think it's hilarious to undermine someone else's confidence under the pretext of 'having a laugh'. But if you let it get to you and give up then you will live a smaller, less adventurous life than you would otherwise. There are times in life when you have to make a stand and let other people know it's not OK to push you around and this is as good an issue as any. Decide that you're only going to discuss your driving with people who are supportive of you. If anyone who isn't brings the subject up then change it briskly. If there are any practical steps you can take to avoid teasing, then do. For example, if your flatmates hang out of the window and jeer when you set off, get your instructor to pick you up round the corner.

I just don't have enough time. Life is so hectic I have real trouble squeezing in my lessons. And as for revising for my theory test – forget it!

Do you have no time because you're a single mum, you're looking after an ill relative or you're juggling your final year at university with holding down two part-time jobs? If so, then yes, you may well be genuinely overstretched and should reconsider whether this is the right time for you to learn to drive. However, maybe the reason you've got no time is because of poor organization or a packed social calendar. If it's the latter, it's worth looking at ways you can use your time more efficiently, such as:

- Instead of reading the paper on your morning commute, study *The Highway Code*.
- If you usually spend Saturday and Sunday mornings groaning with a hangover, then drinking less or having soft drinks on your nights out so you wake up bright and breezy can free up a surprising amount of time. And you could also look upon an evening out spent drinking soft drinks as valuable training for those times when you've got your licence and find you're the chauffeur for the evening.
- If you're a student, draw up a timetable for revising and writing essays and stick to it. By ensuring you're not losing time into the black hole of coffee-bar chat and day-time telly you may discover that you've actually got more of it than you thought.
- Be more assertive when your boss tries to get you to do more overtime.

Basically, it's about deferred gratification. Are you prepared to give up your Saturday lie-in or hectic social life for a while in order for the long-term gain of having a licence and the freedom to drive anywhere you like? It's your call.

L

As you draw closer to your test, you'll find you're becoming more self-reliant and able to make your own decisions. 'You'll have started off as teacher and pupil,' says Dr Peter Russell, Professor of Road Safety, 'and gradually become more like co-drivers.' This is the point at which you're on the final stretch – so congratulations! Turn to Chapters 6 and 7 for advice on how to sharpen up your skills through mock tests, extra practice and tips for dealing with nerves.

Although it's important to make the most of your lessons, you'll progress even faster and learn more thoroughly if you have the chance to practise outside them as well. The following chapter will help you work out who might make a suitable companion and provide vital guidelines for improving your driving without damaging your relationship.

Chapter 4

You're Driving Me Crazy!

Practice might not make perfect but the right sort will definitely help get you through your driving test and cut down the cost of learning to drive. 'The more practice you have, the less lessons you are likely to need,' says driving instructor Chris Pope. 'People who don't get the chance to practise outside lessons at all are likely to need far more, which can make getting up to test standard very expensive.' Another advantage is that you're likely to cover more miles and experience a wider range of driving conditions. However, if you're reading this somewhat wistfully as you suspect you won't be able to rustle up anyone to practise with, don't despair. DSA figures reveal that between a third and a half of successful candidates don't have any practice outside their lessons at all, and they manage to get through. It's just easier if you can get that extra help.

If you're fortunate enough to be able to go out for practice drives, there are some decisions to be made:

- Who are you going to practise with? Your partner, your parents, a helpful friend? Anyone in your social circle with steady nerves and an hour to spare?
- Whose car are you going to use? Are your parents or partner prepared to trust you with their pride and joy? Or would it be best to get a car of your own to practise in?
- Insurance – before you get behind the wheel, you'll need to be insured. The cost can vary dramatically depending on which of the above scenarios you go for, so it's important to research the different options before making any

final decision. (See Chapter 10, 'Car Insurance Without Tears', for more details.)

● And, finally, what do you want to do during your sessions – everyday driving, structured practice, or a combination of the two?

So who loves you enough to sit next to you when you're learning to drive?

Because they're going to have to do it for love, not money. Only qualified driving instructors are allowed to charge for driving tuition. From a legal point of view your companion has to be over twenty-one and have held a licence for the type of car you'll be practising in (manual or automatic) for at least three years. From an emotional and psychological point of view, they have to be someone with whom you have a sufficiently strong relationship that sitting next to you as a learner isn't going to be traumatic for both of you.

'Look at the relationship you have with any potential accompanying driver and any conflicts you have normally,' says Bob Smalley of RoSPA. 'If you tend to argue, be critical of each other or get overemotional and moody then that's likely to be made worse in a driving situation where you're stuck together in a metal box and can't back off or get away from the situation.' And even people who get on well usually can run into problems. 'My own parents had a very har- monious relationship,' says family therapist Denise Knowles. 'But when I was about ten my mother was learning to drive and I can remember my father taking her out for a practice session. They set off and then returned very quickly, both looking furious. My mother was shouting, "You're treating me like I'm stupid", and he was shouting back. I've never heard them raise their voices before or since. The experience made me realize even then that driving practice has the potential to be an emotional minefield.'

You could try an exercise to help you get in tune with what any potential practice companions might really be like to go out driving with. Take a deep breath and imagine a tranquil scene such as a beach or sunset. Let yourself relax into it for a few moments, then let a new scene open up before you. You and your boyfriend/mum/dad are out driving together. Does anyone have a face that is white and taut with terror? Or fury? Does anyone have a stupid, superior smirk on their face as they draw attention to someone else's problems with lane discipline? Is anyone getting out of the car and slamming doors? Is anyone crying? If your intuition is channelling a disturbing vision of what learning to drive with a particular person might be like, then take heed! This is someone it would probably be best to avoid going out practising with, or at least not unless you have a serious heart-to-heart beforehand and sort out any potential problems. Accompanying drivers you might want to avoid include those of a nervous disposition, critical types and ones with bad habits they're not prepared to reform.

Of course, not all problems with practice drives are necessarily down to the person supervising. If there are arguments and scenes during your drives together examine your conscience and ask yourself if maybe you're being too headstrong or emotional. If that's the case, then maybe making every effort to calm down or toughen up will make your sessions easier for both of you.

Practising with family members and partners can work really well

'If you've got the right sort of relationship it can be fantastic,' says family therapist Denise Knowles. 'It's a great opportunity for bonding between parents and children. By helping them practise the parent is saying, "I'm here for you, I'm backing you up", but at the same time helping them become more independent and showing that they're seeing them as an adult.'

> *I was a horrible teenager and was just coming out of that phase of acting as though my parents were useless and knew nothing when it was time to learn to drive. My dad and I had become really distant over the previous few years but he took me out to practise and it was great. We both love cars, so we had this common interest that helped us get to know each other again and rebuild a strong relationship.* Jude, 21

If you've got a relaxed relationship with your partner, your drives together can just be enjoyable, uncomplicated fun – as well as saving you loads of money on extra lessons. If possible, aim to get practice with a variety of people – maybe your partner during the week and then going for weekend drives with your parents. Obviously you'll have to research the insurance implications of this. But just as driving different cars can make you more confident of your ability to handle cars in general, having different people in the passenger seat will help on the journey towards seeing yourself as a 'real driver'.

L

Right, we're raring to go! What do we need to do to get started?

Decide on your practice car

Once you've got your accompanying driver sorted out, you're going to have to decide whether you're going to drive their car or get one of your own to practise in. The main advantage of driving theirs is that it's going to be a lot cheaper; by the time you've added up the cost of buying, taxing, repairing, insuring and running a car of your own you're looking at a pretty hefty bill. On the other hand, driving someone else's car can be a stressful business. Apart from the obvious worry of damaging it, even relatively trivial matters can cause problems.

> *My boyfriend had a flash sports car that was his pride and joy, and when we went out together he absolutely hated having to put 'L' plates on it.* Lucy, 24

You're also limited in that you can only practise when they're available. Whereas if you're in the enviable position of being able to buy your own car to practise in before you've even passed your test then there's more potential for waylaying any suitably qualified friend or family member to go out driving with you. Reading Chapter 10, 'Car Insurance Without Tears', will give you an idea of the costs involved and help you decide if car ownership is the right choice for you at the moment.

It can feel very strange to be driving a car that's different from your instructor's. The fact that it may be a different size, the steering might be heavier or the engine more powerful can all feel unnerving at first. But start off slowly and you'll be fine once you've settled into it. You'll probably also find that driving different vehicles will make you a better all-round driver as it'll give you more of a feel for cars in general.

Prepare your practice car

- ☞ You'll need to display L-plates (or D-plates in Wales) on the front and rear of the car. Make sure that they don't obscure the view and that they're removed or covered when someone who is not a learner is driving.
- ☞ The car has to be roadworthy, taxed, properly insured and if it is over three years old have a valid MOT certificate.
- ☞ It's a good idea to get a temporary interior rear-view mirror for the passenger side to help the accompanying driver see what's happening behind. However, check first with the car manufacturer that it won't interfere with the operation of the air bag. These mirrors are attached via a suction cup and cost about £5. They need to be positioned as close to the left of the main rear-view mirror as possible.

Get your companion(s) to read 'Tips for accompanying a learner' on pp. 63–67

Read it yourself as well, as the information is relevant for both of you.

Finally, you'll need to decide what form you want your practising to take

The two main approaches you can take to practising are: the structured, faux-lesson route where you and your companion focus on aspects of driving you're having the most problems with or just going for general drives. The benefits and problems linked with each approach are outlined below to help you make a decision about which you'd rather go for, or whether you'd prefer a combination of the two. Talk it over with your driving instructor to get their views as well.

General driving – This has got a number of advantages. First, it's a lot easier to multitask with this approach. Rather than your companion having to put aside time to do structured practice, you can go for drives you would have done anyway, such as going to the supermarket, visiting friends or the countryside. And the more time you spend behind the wheel, the more opportunity you'll have to experience different driving situations such as night driving, country driving, and coming across bin lorries, road accidents, crocodiles of schoolchildren and so on. It also provides an opportunity for a more relaxed driving experience. Instead of sitting, sweaty and anxious, next to your instructor carrying out yet another rubbish parallel park you'll have the opportunity to do nice things – and get a highly motivational insight into what fun driving alone will be once you've passed your test.

    You'll get the most out of going down this route if you also use it to start seeing yourself as a 'proper driver'. Although it's tempting to let the experienced person take responsibility, get into the habit of making your own decisions as soon as you're able to. If you're out shopping together, keep an eye out for a parking space yourself rather than expecting them to point you in the right direction. If you're off to Liz and Adam's housewarming party, then check out the route beforehand so you don't have to be guided there. It's all great practice for when you've passed your test and are out by yourself.

Get involved with tasks such as filling up with petrol, checking tyre pressures and getting the car defrosted and into a driveable condition on winter mornings. You'll be doing these things on your own eventually and they'll be a lot easier if you've been shown the ropes by an experienced person beforehand.

The disadvantage of using your practice time to go on general drives is that you can end up avoiding the thing you really need to work on to get you through your test. If you suspect you might do this, then you could spend a bit of time on each drive tackling your particular bugbear. For example, making a detour to tackle your bête-noire roundabout in the run-up to your test, or setting ten minutes aside for a few reverses round a corner.

'I feel that private practice is best spent going on the sort of journeys you'd do normally such as to the supermarket or visiting friends,' says driving consultant Kathy Higgins. 'It can help prepare you for the sort of driving you'll do when you pass. Structured practice is a trickier issue in that there's a greater chance of the accompanying driver passing on any lazy habits. And with systems that involve marking the learner – such as following the DSA Driver's Record approach [see the Reference Section] – the partners and parents just don't have the training to make decisions about this in the way that a driving instructor would have.'

The structured practice approach – The advantage of going for this approach is that, by concentrating on the weaker areas of your driving, there's the potential to bring them up to scratch and be ready for your test sooner. If you decide to take the structured practice option, there are several books and websites that can help you. (See the 'Reference Section' for details.)

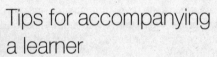

Tips for accompanying a learner

Before setting off

- Make sure you feel positive about going ahead. 'If you're scared by the prospect of being driven by a learner then they'll pick up on your fear and make more mistakes,' says family therapist Denise Knowles. 'Only do it if you want to – not because you feel obliged to. A good way of putting it is to say, "I don't feel confident enough in my own abilities to sit in with you." Or set out your boundaries in advance – for example, you might feel OK about practising in a deserted car park, but want to draw the line at bombing along a busy dual carriageway.' The 'deserted car park' option might also be best if the learner will be driving your car and you're worried about them damaging it. However, do be willing to keep an open mind in both of these cases. You may well develop rather more faith in the learner as they come up to test standard and be prepared to venture further afield with them.

- You'll need to have held a full licence for the practice car (manual or automatic) for at least three years and be over twenty-one. Although it's not a legal requirement, having a responsible attitude to driving and no points on your licence is also going to make you a better prospect as a practice companion.

- Remember that rules like the drink-drive laws and the ban on using a hand-held mobile when driving apply to anyone supervising a learner. Although you're not the one behind the wheel, you're officially 'in control' of the vehicle, so getting your learner-driver girlfriend to drive you back from a boozy night at the pub isn't an option. However, if they're caught going over the speed limit the points will go on their licence not yours – though you could also be prosecuted for aiding and abetting an offence.

- Read the latest edition of *The Highway Code* to refresh your memory and catch up on any changes.

- 'It's worth taking one of our Experienced Driver Assessments [EDA],' says Bob Smalley of RoSPA. 'The assessment is one hour long and costs thirty-five pounds excluding VAT. Assessors are registered with the RoSPA Advanced Drivers' Association and at the end you're given a completely confidential verbal and written assessment of your driving ability and advice on any areas you might need to brush up on in order to avoid passing on any bad habits.' The course is available throughout the UK as an assessor will travel to meet you at a convenient location. (See the RoSPA website for details.)

- Or you might want to consider going out for a refresher training session with the learner's instructor. If you were in France you'd have to! There it's compulsory for practice companions to have three hours' instruction to bring them up to standard before they're allowed to accompany a learner. If you're the parent of a younger learner, this would also be a good opportunity to discreetly vet the instructor to check out their teaching methods and their approach to dealing with traffic and ensure that they're not likely to behave inappropriately with your daughter!

- If you're not able to do either of the above, do at least have a chat with the learner's instructor or sit in the back during a regular lesson. The instructor can bring you up to date with the style of driving that's currently required to reach test standard and tell you what areas your learner needs to work on. And don't let this conversation be a one-off – keep in regular contact throughout the learning process.
- Another point to consider if you're in someone else's car is whether you're insured to drive it back if the learner feels ill or has a scary experience that makes her lose her nerve. Your own insurance may cover you to drive other people's cars with their permission, so check that out first. If not, you might want to look into being put on their insurance.
- If you're driving in the learner's car rather than your own, take time to check out the instrument panel before setting off so you know where the headlamps, hazard lights and so on are and can point them out quickly to the learner if they're dithering – or lean over and operate them yourself if necessary.
- Avoid having children as passengers as they can distract the learner's attention.

On the road

- Don't attempt anything new until the driving instructor has taught it first. And wait until the learner has been taught the emergency stop before you take them out on the public roads.
- Think through the route you're planning to take beforehand and make sure it's at the right level for your learner. At the very start it would be best to drive them somewhere quiet such as a car park or housing estate before swapping over and letting

them take the wheel. And as things progress, err on the side of caution when planning routes. If you're going into the town centre with them for the first time and one approach involves a big scary roundabout and the other doesn't, it's probably better to take the latter route initially rather face a panicky, 'Oh God no, I can't stand this roundabout!' scenario just as you're bearing down on it.

- Remember that without dual controls the only way you have of controlling the car is through your voice – by telling your learner clearly what they need to do. Don't see the handbrake as a backup for stopping the car if you need to. If it's used at speeds over 15 m.p.h. it could send the car into a skid that the learner wouldn't know how to cope with. Stick to unchallenging routes until the instructor tells you the learner can be trusted with more ambitious ones.

- Regardless of your own usual driving style, encourage a responsible and safety-conscious approach in your learner. This isn't the time for a Jeremy-Clarksonesque rant about speed cameras.

- Always give directions well in advance. Be clear and specific and give backup instructions, too, if you can. For example, 'Take first turn right, the one that's signposted for the swimming pool.'

- If the learner takes a wrong turn, don't panic or give a sudden change of direction. Get them to drive on and work your way back to your original route when it's convenient.

- Encourage the learner to check their speed and keep an eye on it yourself too, as inexperienced drivers can easily forget.

- Remind them to check their mirrors regularly.

- Remember that learners aren't allowed on the motorway.

- You can use the drives to work on hazard perception and road signs as you're going along. Point out signs and ask them what they mean – you might find you need to refer to *The Highway Code* to remind yourself of some of them.

- Be calm and positive about the learner's driving. When giving feedback one training method is the 'bad news sandwich' – giving praise, then constructive criticism, and then praise again. Another is 'better, and better again' where you point out something they've done well, and then how it could be improved. For example, 'You handled that roundabout well, but to make it even better you could have checked your mirrors more frequently.'
- If the learner does do something dangerous during the drive, try to stay calm. Then as soon as you can, get them to pull over somewhere safe and discuss it.
- If there's any feedback you want to give about the learner's driving at the end of the session, discuss it in the car, then close the door and leave it behind you.
- Don't underestimate the importance of just chatting about driving. Sharing experiences about when you got boxed into a parking space or how you handled your first long-distance drive can both narrow the gulf between you and provide useful tips. It also helps the learner see that driving isn't about making some mysterious transition from being a 'hopeless learner' to a 'perfect licensed driver' but more a continuum where learning to cope with new driving situations is a process that keeps happening long after the test itself is a distant memory.

Driving alone as a learner

Don't even think of going out on practice drives by yourself! Driving alone before you've passed your test is dangerous and irresponsible. But unfortunately it is quite widespread. 'It's estimated that approximately one in twenty drivers is unlicensed, either because they've been banned or because they haven't yet passed their test,' says driving consultant Kathy Higgins. 'And I've had pupils who claim to have only been out for a few sessions with friends but I can tell have been driving alone for years – they're so confident on the road there couldn't be any other explanation.'

If you get stopped by the police you will end up with points on your licence before you've even passed your test and will be fined as well. Also, by driving alone as a learner you render any insurance you might have invalid. This means that if you damage something or (even worse) injure someone you could be sued and spend the foreseeable future paying it off.

In 2005 a 37-year-old learner driver from Scotland came up with what she obviously thought was a cunning plan that would fool other drivers into thinking she had a companion. She dressed up an inflatable dummy used for demonstrating first aid and placed it in the passenger seat. It didn't work though, she was stopped by police and given six points on her provisional licence and a £1000 fine.

L

Driving with a professional instructor can be a very formal experience. Practising with someone else will give you a much greater feel for everyday driving. And as well as providing useful experience gives you an added incentive to stick at it and get that licence!

Chapter 5

The Theory Test

The theory test is a rubbish name for a test. Unlike the practical test, which does actually sound as if it's going to be useful, the theory test brings to mind quantum mechanics, logarithms and that thing about the sum of the square of the hypotenuse being equal to the sum of the other two sides. The sort of stuff that Stephen Hawking needs to keep up to date with, but not your average person.

It should be called something like the 'How To Drive Without Killing Yourself Or Other People Or Racking Up Loads Of Parking Tickets Test' because that's what it's really about. Knowing the rules of the road and understanding road signs is vital for safe driving. However, many learners see the theory test as something to just get out of the way en route to the more challenging business of passing their practical.

I found it very straighforward. Most of the multiple choice questions are common sense and the hazard perception part is fine if you just practise with the DVD beforehand so you know what they're after. Narinder, 20

The theory test is ridiculously easy, and the hazard perception part is just ridiculous. Hannah, 18

The theory test isn't particularly difficult but the national pass rate for 2004/5 was only 64 per cent. This is because many people think that most of the questions will be a matter of common sense and don't bother revising. However, there are enough about technical matters such as road markings and traffic signs to mean that you'll fail if you don't study properly beforehand. It's also important to prepare for it with an attitude of really wanting to become a knowledgeable and skilful driver, rather than seeing it as something to cram for and then be forgotten the moment you get your pass certificate. Whether it's dealing with a major incident like breaking down on the motorway, an everyday driving issue such as knowing what child restraints are needed for different heights and age groups, or recognizing an unusual sign – such as the one showing a cute puffing train that looks as though it could involve directions to a steam train museum but is actually a warning of a level crossing without a barrier ahead – this is vital information for your future as a licensed driver, so it's important to absorb it thoroughly.

It's also a good idea to see it as an opportunity to give serious thought to what sort of driver you're going to be once you've passed your test. After all, there's not much point in being able to rattle off stopping distances as easily as your two times table, if you then go on to drive up everyone's backside once you're on the road.

In everyday life most mistakes can be put right, but when you're driving a mistake like drinking too much, talking on your mobile or speeding can mean the difference between life and death – your own or someone else's. And although it's tempting to tune out all those harrowing TV adverts about drink driving, cellophane-wrapped bunches of carnations tied to railings at accident blackspots or the scary statistics – for example, the Department for Transport road casualties 2004 report which reveals that we all have a one in 200 chance of dying on the roads – with an 'it won't happen to me' attitude, the fact is that you owe it to yourself and others to be as safe as you can. Having not just a knowledge of the rules of the road, but also a commitment to putting them into practice is essential.

Recognizing road signs

A survey of 524 drivers carried out in 2005 by motorinsurance.co.uk found none could name all twelve of a selection of common road signs. The recognition level was worst for hazard signs. Only 42 per cent recognized the slippery roads sign, while only 23 per cent knew the uneven road surface sign and only 8 per cent identified the side winds signs. However, 100 per cent recognized the sign for speed cameras (which looks very like one anyway). Many motoring organizations expressed concern about the findings, including Neil Greig, Head of Policy for the AA Motoring Trust in Scotland. He also made the point that 'We need a *Highway Code* that will tempt people to reread it, because hardly anyone does so after they have passed their driving test. It is such a boring document and should be made more readable and user-friendly.' Mr Greig suggested that leaflets reminding motorists about road signs could be sent out with tax-disc renewal forms.

The test itself

You have to pass the theory test before you're allowed to book and take your practical test. You can only book one theory test at a time, so if you fail you'll have to wait to rebook another one. If you didn't pass it was because you weren't fully prepared, so the DSA guidelines state that you must leave it three working days before taking it again. Most driving instructors advise that the best time to take your theory test is after you've had a few lessons, so you're familiar with being on the road and can apply what you're learning to practical situations. The theory test is a computer-based test and consists of two parts: multiple choice and hazard perception. You need to pass both sections at the same time; if you fail one section you'll have to take the whole test again.

The multiple choice test

This is a test in which you answer questions on road signs, the rules of the road and good driving practice using a computer. The questions are chosen from a bank of about 1000. As of January 2012 the actual questions have not been published but similar ones are available in Focus Multimedia products and you should revise with these aids so you'll be familiar with them. One of the questions will be based on a 'case study' scenario which involves a short story on which five multiple choice questions will be based. In the future the DSA may introduce more case study questions to the test.

The test takes place in a room full of computer stations where there will be other candidates who have all started the test at different times. You're given the chance to practise answering some sample questions before you begin the test properly. You're then allowed up to fifty-seven minutes and to pass you must answer at least forty-three out of fifty questions correctly. You select your answers by touching buttons on the screen. Some questions may ask for two or more correct answers from a selection. If you're unsure about some questions you can mark them with a flag to help you go back to them. You can also review your test and change any answers you've given right up until the end of the test.

It's a good idea to answer the easy questions first, it'll build up your confidence. Then you can go back and tackle the trickier ones. Many people report having whizzed through their multiple choice questions in no time, but don't feel self-conscious about taking the test slowly and carefully however straightforward it may seem. But even if you feel fairly confident about your answers, it's worth taking that extra time to go over them all again. Some questions can be deceptively simple and at first glance it's easy to choose the wrong answer, but a second look will pick this up. After all, a few extra minutes could make the difference between passing or having to go through the inconvenience and expense of taking it again.

Break

You're allowed to take a break of up to three minutes before moving on to the next section, though you're not allowed to leave your seat during it.

The hazard perception test

New drivers have a much higher risk of accidents and the aim of the hazard perception test is to increase their skills at reading the road and recognizing as early as possible any clues which show a dangerous situation might be about to develop. It was introduced as part of the theory test in November 2002.

What is the format? – The test takes about twenty minutes and consists of fourteen video clips, each about one minute long. Before you start this part of the test you'll be shown a short tutorial video which explains how the test works and gives you the opportunity to watch a sample video clip. Each clip will show, from the driver's point of view, everyday road scenes and developing hazards of various types. You need to press your mouse button as soon as you see a 'developing hazard'. A developing hazard is defined as something that may result in the driver having to take some action, such as changing speed or direction. You don't need to move the mouse to where the hazard is and you can left or right click. When you click the clip won't stop or slow down but a red flag will appear at the bottom of the screen to show your response has been recorded.

Examples of developing hazards include the sort of things you come across every day when driving. Thinking of them as 'a potential problem' might give you a clearer idea of what they cover:

- A pedestrian about to cross the road.
- A car emerging from a junction on the left.
- A parked car getting ready to pull out.
- A van turning right across the traffic.
- A green traffic light that changes as you approach it.
- Roadworks.

You are given a 'window of time' of a few seconds in which to respond to the hazard by clicking the mouse. The earlier you spot the potential danger and respond the higher your score. You won't score any points if you respond outside the 'window of time'. However, some people believe that experienced road users tend to see the potential problem in advance and click before the official 'scoring window' opens, thus scoring nothing for that clip.

About how many clicks should I do? – As there will be only one, or at most two, scorable hazards in the clip it's easy to feel that you should only click once or twice. However, it's better to click more frequently as it's easy to be unsure which 'hazard' they're focusing on, or at which point they really feel you should be spotting it. However, if you click too often it can be interpreted as cheating, and a 'You have responded to this clip in an unacceptable manner' message will come up. You'll then score nothing for that clip. 'You should be OK with several clicks per hazard as long as you don't click rhythmically,' says driving consultant Kathy Higgins. 'Don't overanalyse the clip, just click if you see something hazardous, then click again.' The best way to check if you're getting it right is to practise in advance with the hazard perception study aids, which will give you feedback on your performance.

How is it scored? – There are a total of fifteen scorable hazards. Thirteen clips contain one scorable hazard and one clip contains two of them. You can score up to five marks for each hazard depending on how quickly you identify it. Unlike the multiple choice, in this section you're not allowed to go back or change your response. The pass mark for the hazard perception test is forty-four out of seventy-five points.

L

The hazard perception test has attracted a certain amount of negative press from driving professionals. Some feel that it's too much like a computer game and that hazard perception skills are best taught out on lessons with an instructor. Others feel that the format only suits novice road users and that those with more experience (such as motorcyclists) are more likely to fail it. That's why making several clicks per hazard can be a good idea because even if the first one is 'too early' the others will be noted within the 'scoring window'. This all sounds very complicated, I know. But it's really not something to get your knickers in a twist about. Most learners have no problems passing, as although the hazard perception test is hard to explain and hard to imagine before you've taken it, you'll find it's very straightforward when you come to do it. And if you've prepared properly with the help of the Focus Multimedia study aids you'll be fine.

> *Driving instructors are required to take this test and in mine I got fifty-eight, whereas my daughter, who took it the day after her seventeenth birthday, having only had one lesson, scored sixty-four! Some learners who've been cyclists or motorcyclists fail the test because they're 'too good for it' and have to 'dumb down' a bit in order to get through.* Tony Friday, driving instructor

Revising for your theory test

A sample study carried out by the Df T in 2004 showed that the average amount of time spent studying for the theory test is 15.3 hours for women, 12.2 for men. It's essential to thoroughly memorize *The Highway Code* and also to use the other study aids listed in the 'Reference Section'.

How to learn most effectively

It's been proved that the best way to take information in and make sure it sticks is to learn it through a variety of different routes, including visual (seeing and reading), auditory (hearing), oral (speaking), feeling and doing. This way the information becomes more strongly 'encoded' in the brain and becomes easier to remember. Here are some ways you could use this approach to help you prepare for your theory test.

Visual

• An excellent way to revise is to download the questions supplied by Focus Multimedia onto your iPhone, iPad or iPad Touch. You can then revise any time, anywhere. Refer to it while you're waiting in a queue, on the bus or taking a coffee break. Bookmark any questions you find difficult so you can refer back to them.

• Get your family and friends to test you by asking you to draw the different signs, for example the national speed limit applies or no waiting ones. This works really well because it means you have actually to remember what the sign looks like, rather than just recognize it.

• Learning the history behind the road signs can help you remember them. Britain's road signs were designed by graphic designers Jock Kinneir and Margaret Calvert in the mid-1960s to replace the confusing mix of signs that had existed beforehand. Their system is seen as a design classic and has become a role model for modern road signage all over the world. Margaret based several of the images on aspects of her own life; for example, the school sign in which a girl leads a little boy is drawn from a photograph of herself as a child, and the cow in the farm animals warning sign was Patience, a cow on her relatives' farm in Wiltshire!

Auditory and oral

• Get a friend or your mum to ask you questions from the theory test book.

• When you're studying the theory test materials, say bits you have trouble remembering out loud; for example, 'Loading restrictions are shown by yellow marks on the kerb.' Try repeating stopping distances to yourself (doing this on the bus can get you some funny looks so you might prefer to wait until you're by yourself).

- Record yourself describing road signs or the rules of the road, then plug in your earphones and listen to it as you're walking along.
- 'Commentary driving' can be helpful. This is where you talk about what you're seeing as you're driving along; for example, 'We are now joining a dual carriageway where the speed limit is 70 m.p.h.' or 'We are now entering a one-way street.' It's best to start doing it as a passenger (with an understanding driver).
- Talk about driving behaviour and hazard awareness with friends and family. Encourage them to tell you anecdotes about how they handled breaking down on the motorway or the time they got a parking ticket because they didn't understand the regulations properly; it'll help you relate your learning to everyday life.

Remembered emotion

- When you're looking at the questions related to parking, summon up the trauma you'd experience if you parked in the wrong place and got a ticket.
- If you're the sort of driver who likes to put their foot down, then think of the sense of freedom you'll feel when moving out of a built-up area and seeing the national speed limit applies sign.
- Visualize yourself hearing the siren of a police car behind you. Instead of panicking, you move confidently to the side of the road to let them through.
- Or you could imagine yourself stuck in a traffic jam and then the sense of delight you'll feel when you realise that it's now just past the time when it's OK to move over and use the adjacent bus lane.

The remembered emotion approach also provides a good opportunity to do some hard thinking about the questions where the actual answer is easy, but carrying it out in real life can be potentially more challenging. For example, how does alcohol affect you?

1. It speeds up your reactions
2. It increases your awareness
3. It improves your co-ordination
4. It reduces your co-ordination

You chose the last one? No surprises there then. Like many of the theory test questions, it's down to common sense. But although getting the right answer to questions like this isn't too difficult, what really matters is putting it into practice. If you're going to a party and planning to drive, will you really be OK about sticking to soft drinks? Even if you don't know many people and you know a glass of wine would help you relax? Even if that bloke you've fancied for ages turns up and you're desperate for a spot of Dutch courage before you go over to talk to him? If the answer to these other, real-life questions is 'no' or 'not sure', then maybe this is a good time to decide that you'll always have a policy of leaving the car at home and getting a lift or a taxi when you go for a night out. The same goes for questions about speeding or using a mobile phone. Make a commitment to keep your phone switched off when you're driving and always respect the speed limit.

Activity
- When you're out driving with your instructor or on a practice drive, make a point of noting the road signs or markings you've learnt. And if there are ones you don't

recognize, ask your instructor or companion what they mean.

- When you're a passenger in a car or bus actively engage with what's happening on the road. Look out for the bus lanes, the speed limits, when you come up to some traffic lights test yourself on what colour they're likely to turn next.

- Pay particular attention when you're on unfamiliar routes. If you're a city girl then a trip to the countryside will give you the chance to see new road signs (like that one with the deer running across the road – not many of those round Tooting Broadway), and get used to the correct etiquette around tractors.

- The multiple choice section includes a subsection on documents. If you've got a car, get out the file containing the relevant paperwork. Go through the insurance documents, MOT certificate and so on to remind yourself of the details. If you don't have a car, then ask to borrow the car file belonging to your parents or partner.

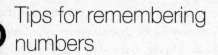

Tips for remembering numbers

Several of the questions in the multiple choice section involve remembering numbers. For example:

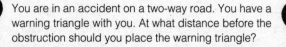

You are in an accident on a two-way road. You have a warning triangle with you. At what distance before the obstruction should you place the warning triangle?

1. 25 metres (82 feet)
2. 45 metres (148 feet)
3. 100 metres (328 feet)
4. 150 metres (492 feet)

The correct answer is 45 metres (148 feet). When studying a question like this, ask yourself if there's anything about the number 45 that could help make it stick in your mind? Maybe it's your mum's age, or the number of the bus into town, or a flat you've lived in? Or if you're into counting calories you might remember that there are 45 in a Jaffa cake or an apple. Linking numbers with other things in this way can help you remember them.

Revising for the hazard perception part of the test

Talking about hazard perception with your driving instructor can be helpful. But the best way to prepare for the hazard perception section is to use the study aids, which contain video clips similar to those you'll see when you take your test, and also show you the correct time to respond.

Booking your theory test

There are over 150 test centres in the UK and most people have one within twenty miles of their home. Your instructor will tell you where your nearest one is. You can take the test on weekdays, evenings and on Saturdays. You can book your test by phone, online or by post. If you prefer to book by post you'll need to fill in an application form which is available from theory test centres or driving test centres. You should receive a letter confirming your appointment within ten days. If you need to cancel or postpone your test you have to give at least three working days' notice or you forfeit the fee. If you have dyslexia, would prefer to take the test in a language other than English, have hearing problems or other special needs let the DSA know at the time of booking and arrangements can be made to accommodate you.

The day of your theory test

For most people the theory test doesn't cause anything like the same anxiety levels or sleep loss as the practical one. But if the prospect of sitting the exam does leave you feeling anxious then dip into the sections on tackling nerves in Chapter 7 for some useful tips.

On the day you'll need to bring your signed photocard licence and paper counterpart and your appointment card or booking number. If you forget them you won't be allowed to take the test and you'll lose the fee. It's also important to arrive in plenty of time.

The test result

After completing both the multiple choice and hazard perception tests you should receive your score for both within ten minutes. If you're told you've failed, then commiserations. You're bound to feel disappointed. And frustrated too, if you've passed on one section and not the other. But if that's the case at least you now know where your weakness lies and what you need to focus on for success next time. You might be eager to take your test again as soon as you can (the earliest allowed is at least three working days later) or you may prefer more time for revision. Talking it over with your driving instructor will help you decide on the right approach.

If you've passed – congratulations! You'll be given a pass certificate, which is valid for two years. If you don't pass your practical test within this time you'll have to retake your theory test. You'll need to quote the number when you book your practical test and you must take the certificate with you when you attend. And if you're still at a stage where you're struggling with the practical side, then really let yourself celebrate this success. Buy yourself something nice, treat yourself to lunch out or get together with some friends. Applying what you've learnt in your lessons and practice sessions will help you become more confident on the road and help you on your way to your future practical test triumph!

Chapter 6

The Final Stretch

Sometimes it happens in a blinding flash, but often it dawns on you more slowly. You feel less sweaty and humiliated by your attempts at parking. Your driving instructor is taking you on more demanding routes and you're coping with them fine. He doesn't have to sort out major mistakes so much and the emphasis during lessons is more about fine-tuning your skills. And then you realize that's because you've become more capable. You're turning into a Real Driver. Someone who you can imagine as having a licence and being allowed to drive places by themselves. By this point you'll probably start feeling that you're ready to take your test, your driving instructor will feel the same and you'll get things moving. But there are a couple of other possible scenarios.

I reckon I'm ready for my test but my instructor won't let me take it yet. Is he refusing because he wants to keep my money coming in? Also, I know he's got a real ego thing about his high first-time pass rate. Maybe he's worried that I'll fail and bring it down?

If you've got a good instructor, the chances are that he'll already have new pupils on his waiting list and far from wanting to hang on to you, he'll be just as keen to move on himself. So if your instructor doesn't want to put you in for your test the most likely reason is because he doesn't think you're up to it yet. If you've been working with a Driver's Record he can show you where you haven't reached level 5 in all twenty-four key skills (able to carry them out consistently without any prompting) and tell you what you need to do to improve. Remember, being able to drive well consistently is really important; the roads are getting busier and more demanding all the time and you're not ready to be let loose on them until you're truly capable – having a few good days isn't enough. And as far as the ego stuff goes – driving instructors are aware that how you perform on test is going to reflect on them. Driving instructors have a professional responsibility not to put their pupils up for their test until they're ready. If an instructor is regularly putting through candidates of a poor standard they could end up being questioned by the DSA. However, if you really have reason to suspect your driving instructor is taking advantage of you, then book a lesson with someone else and ask them for a second opinion.

I need to get my licence straight away so I can drive to work. Couldn't I just take my test and see if I can scrape through?
This isn't a good idea. 'Your aim should be to become a safe driver in the long term, not to have the minimum number of lessons and then have a crack at your test,' says Kevin Delaney, Traffic and Road Safety Manager at the Royal Automobile Club (RAC) Foundation. 'It's not like cramming for a French exam and seeing if you can manage a pass. After all, if you make a bad mistake when speaking French you might risk feeling foolish or embarrassed, but if you make a bad driving mistake you could kill yourself or someone else.'

If the pressure is on for you to pass quickly then aim to spend as much time behind the wheel as you can to build up your skills and confidence. Get all the practice you can squeeze in and have more frequent lessons.

Being told that you're up to standard by your driving instructor is fantastic.

My instructor got me to do a parallel park and turn the engine off. Then he turned to me and said, 'I think you're ready to take your test.' It was such an amazing moment. I'd struggled with driving for so long I'd got to the point where I thought they were words I'd long for but never hear, like news I'd won the lottery or George Clooney asking me to marry him.
Eva, 33

Choosing the time and date of your practical test

Once it's been decided that you're ready for your test you'll have to sort out a mutually convenient date and time with your instructor. If you're taking the test in your instructor's car, you'll need him to be available. But even if you're taking it in your own car it's still best if he's able to give you a lesson and pep talk before the test, sit in on the post-test analysis with your examiner (the feedback will be useful whether you pass or fail), and take you home afterwards.

Here are some tips for choosing the right date and time for your test:

- Try not to have it too near another major life event like exams, moving house or getting married.
- Taking your test in the morning gives less time for nerves to build up.
- If you get stressed driving in the rush hour you might like to book your test at a quieter time of day.
- It's possible to have a friend, relative or your instructor sit in on your test, though they're not allowed to make any input. If you think you'd find it embarrassing or offputting,

then obviously that wouldn't be a good idea. But you could find having someone there who's 'on your team' and supporting you helpful for calming nerves. If you decide to be accompanied you don't have to arrange it beforehand; the person can just introduce themselves to the examiner at the test centre. However, you will have to check with them at this point and make sure you find a date that's suitable for both of you.

- If you find it difficult to get time off work or college during the week it is possible to book weekend tests and also ones during summer evenings, but they are more expensive.

To tell or not to tell?

Once you've decided on the date of your test, think carefully before you announce it to your family, friends and colleagues. You might feel better only telling people closest to you, or maybe even no one at all. It can help keep the pressure of other people's expectations down and means that you can surprise everyone when you tell them you've passed!

Taking the test in your practice car

Once they're driving their practice car some people decide they'd like to be taught in it and take their test in it as well. If you're keen to do this discuss it with your driving instructor, but there are quite a few reasons why it might not be a good idea. Firstly, it's going to prove more expensive as it's unlikely that the instructor would accept a cut in his lesson fee for taking you in your own car, which means that you'll be paying for the petrol and any wear and tear. It can also be a tricky issue from the point of view of insurance. You'd either have to contact your own insurance company to see if they were willing to cover this or your driving instructor would have to get his insurance extended to teach you in your car.

There's also the fact that your car won't have dual controls and many driving instructors feel they're able to give better and safer tuition in a car that's fitted with them. 'It means I can encourage pupils to make their own decisions at roundabouts and junctions because I know I can take charge if things go wrong,' says driving instructor Chris Pope. Bear in mind, too, that many driving examiners are currently campaigning for a move for dual-controlled cars to be compulsory during tests. A survey carried out in 2005 by the DSA revealed that 95 per cent of tests are currently taken in dual-controlled cars. However, the 5 per cent that aren't are eighty-two times more likely to have the test terminated because the examinee is driving dangerously. This is thought to be because people who don't attend in driving-school cars might not have had any professional instruction at all and have been taught by family and friends instead – and hence be quite some way off the required standard.

Even though you won't be discriminated against for turning up in your own car, you might decide that it doesn't give the best possible impression. If you do decide to go ahead and use your own car you'll need to check the passenger seat belt works, remove any beaded seat covers from the front passenger seat and ensure that there's a head restraint fitted to it. You'll also need to provide an extra interior rear-view mirror for the examiner and fix L-plates front and rear. If you overlook any of these your test will be cancelled and you'll lose your fee.

How to book your test

Test waiting lists are usually about six weeks if you want a particular date and time. If, however, you and your instructor are able to be flexible and accept cancellations it can be quicker than this.

Booking online or on the phone

If you contact the DSA and book by either of these methods you'll be given the time and date of your test immediately. You'll need to tell them what sort of test you want to book and provide:

- your driver number, which is shown on your provisional licence;
- your theory test pass certificate number;
- your driving instructor's code number (your instructor will give you this);
- your credit/debit card details.

You'll be given a booking number and sent an appointment letter within a few days.

L

Booking by post

You can get the application form from driving test centres or your driving instructor. Send it together with the correct fee to the address shown on the back of the form. Don't forget to give your preferred date when you book. You may pay by cheque, postal order or with a credit/debit card and will receive an appointment letter within ten days. If you haven't received your appointment letter after two weeks, then call again to check that everything is in order.

Disabilities and special circumstances

If you have a disability or if there are other special circumstances, you need to let the DSA know when you book your test. More time is allowed for the test so that your examiner can talk to you about your disability and any adaptations fitted to your vehicle.

If the person taking the test can't speak English or is deaf they are allowed to bring an interpreter (who must not be an instructor). The interpreter must be sixteen years or over.

Postponing or cancelling your test

If after booking your test you then need to postpone or cancel it, you'll need to give at least ten working days' notice or you'll lose your fee.

L

Bad weather conditions

If the weather is very bad on the day of your test it may be cancelled. Call the number on your appointment letter to check if your test is going ahead.

Moving things up a gear

As your test approaches, the more time you can spend behind the wheel the better. Extra lessons are a worthwhile investment, maybe even one each day in the final week if you can afford it, as is getting your family or partner to take you out for more practice. This might require heavy-duty begging and pleading, as the novelty value will probably have worn off by now. It's also a good idea to waylay them when they're off on mundane trips and offer to drive. It might mean tearing yourself away from your favourite TV programme to go on a not particularly riveting outing, but it's important to remember that all practice is good practice, especially now.

Mock tests

In the run-up to your practical test, your instructor will probably offer you several 'mock tests'. These are 'pretend tests' as opposed to ones where your instructor and passers-by criticize, laugh, jeer and make hurtful personal remarks. Ideally, a mock test will start and finish at your test centre and be the same length of time as a real test, to help you get a feel for the experience. Your instructor will do the role-play thing and behave as if he were an examiner throughout. That means he'll give you directions but not guidance and mark you on your driving. If you usually chat during lessons with your instructor, expect that to be reduced as the aim is to try to reproduce the more formal atmosphere of the test. It can be really helpful to arrange for another instructor to take at least one of your mock tests, so you get used to having someone unfamiliar in the car. This is particularly useful if you get paranoid about the idea of a stranger watching your every move, as it'll help desensitize you. At the end of the test you'll be told whether you would have passed or failed if that had been your real driving test, and any faults you've made will be discussed and suggestions given to help you perform better in future. Hopefully, you'll get some passes to lift your spirits, but even if you don't you shouldn't be disheartened. Aim to learn from the failures and remember that your instructor wouldn't be allowing you to take your test if you weren't capable of succeeding.

The practical test and what it involves

Your driving instructor will explain the format of the practical test to you in detail. Currently the format of the test is as follows:

Sorting out the paperwork

You'll need to bring the following documents with you. They all need to be originals as the DSA can't accept photocopies.

- Your provisional driving licence, both the photocard and paper counterpart. If you have an old-style paper licence you'll have to bring that together with a valid passport.
- Your theory test pass certificate.
- Your appointment letter.
- If you've been keeping a Driver's Record it's a good idea (though not essential) to bring that as well.

On meeting your examiner you'll be asked to sign a form to confirm that your car insurance is in order. When dealing with paperwork it's important to make sure any money you might have with you won't be visible to the examiner, as this could be taken as an attempt to bribe him and the test would be called off. 'Examiners are very strict on this,' says driving consultant Kathy Higgins. 'Some instructors carry loose change in the ashtray, so it's best to get that out of sight before the test as well.'

Eyesight test

Before you get into your car the examiner will ask you to read a number plate on a vehicle. If it's one with an old-style number plate the required distance is 20.5 metres (about 67 feet). Number plates with a narrower font, such as the new-style number plates introduced in 2001, need to be read from a distance of 20 metres (66 feet). If you wear glasses or contact lenses to do this, you'll be expected to keep them on during the test.

Kicking off with something low-key like this feels good as it eases you into test mode gently and gives your nerves a chance to settle down. By the time you're walking over to your car you should be feeling a bit calmer.

Safety checks

This is also sometimes called 'Show me/Tell me'. In this part of the test you're asked to identify various parts of the engine and demonstrate how you would carry out basic checks and maintenance such as topping up coolant, brake fluid, oil and washer fluid, checking tyres, lights and brakes. It's sort of car maintenance lite in that you just have to point and give explanations in an air-hostess sort of way, rather than roll up your sleeves and change a wheel or anything. Your instructor should have been taking you through all these in the course of your lessons, so hopefully you'll breeze through this stage. You are usually asked one of each of the following:

To show how you would carry out certain safety checks. For example, 'Show me how you would check the headlights and tail lights are working.'
To tell the examiner how you would carry out certain safety checks. For example, 'Tell me how you would check the tyres to ensure they have sufficient tread depth.'

There are only a limited number of safety questions you can be asked on your test and they can all be found on the DSA website. It's possible to get a driving fault for getting the answers wrong, but at the moment you can't be given a major fault, so it's not possible to fail your test on this section.

The practical test

For most learners this represents the pinnacle of scariness. But it's really not that bad. It's just a drive of about forty minutes a manoeuvre and possibly an emergency stop. It'll be shorter than one of your lessons. And the examiner isn't expecting perfection; you're allowed to make faults and still pass. Just drive as well as you have been in your lessons and you'll be fine!

You'll be asked to carry out one of the first three manoeuvres below. Your examiner will ask you to pull over, explain the exercise and ask you to do it. The manoeuvres are:

1. Reversing round a corner.
2. Turning in the road.
3. A reverse parking manoeuvre.
4. In addition, you may also be asked to carry out an emergency stop.

In October 2010 a new section of 'independent driving' was introduced to the practical test. This lasts about 10 minutes and during it you have to drive without step-by-step instructions from the examiner. Instead, they'll ask you to drive by either following road signs and markings or by following a series of verbal directions. It's not a test of your navigational skills and you won't fail if you take the wrong turning. You're also free to ask the examiner to repeat the instructions at any time.

To pass your driving test you need to drive without making any major faults at all. However, you're allowed up to fifteen driving faults (sixteen or more results in failure). Driving faults are what used to be called 'minors'. This is a low-risk fault. For example, if you performed the appropriate observations before pulling out at a junction but still slightly misjudged the distance of an approaching vehicle, causing it to slow down.

Major faults fall into two categories:

1. **Serious faults** – these are faults that weren't dangerous on this occasion but could be in other circumstances and also include 'bad habit' driving faults. For example, if you didn't do proper observations before pulling out at a junction and an approaching vehicle had to slow down significantly.
2. **Dangerous fault** – is one that causes actual danger during the test. For example, if you didn't do proper observations and completely misjudged the speed and distance of an approaching vehicle and the examiner had to take action to avoid a crash.

The examiner may have a supervising examiner sitting in with them. If this happens with you don't worry. The extra examiner isn't there to judge you, but to observe your examiner.

Most people find that the test passes in a blur and actually feels like much less than forty minutes. At the end you'll return to the test centre. This is usually followed by an agonizingly long few seconds while the examiner completes the relevant paperwork and they'll then tell you if you've passed or failed. You'll also be given a driving test report form, which shows any faults and includes notes to explain the report. Whether you've passed or failed, remember that your driving instructor should sit in on the feedback from your examiner. And whatever your result, it's also a good idea to have either your instructor or a friend or relative drive you home; you're likely to be too wound up to be at your best behind the wheel!

The ten most common reasons for driving test failure

As reported by the DSA for the twelve months to January 2004

1. Observation at junctions – ineffective observation and judgement

Aargh! So many of us have problems with junctions and with roundabouts in particular. Unless it's completely clear the decision to pull out can seem agonizingly fraught. If you nip into the first half-decent gap will you be seen as reckless and overimpulsive? But then if you wait for a bigger one maybe you'll be penalized for hesitancy. Such internal wranglings aren't particularly productive to taking quick and appropriate action, so your best strategy is to forget about second-guessing what your examiner might be thinking, trust your own judgement and drive as you have been during your lessons.

2. Reverse parking – ineffective observation or a lack of accuracy

Carrying out a reverse park requires good car control and observational skills and under test conditions it's easy to get flummoxed. Staying calm and taking your time will help you get it right. If the car seems to be going wide or too close to the kerb, then don't panic and assume you've messed it up. By thinking things through you can still complete the manoeuvre successfully.

3. Use of mirrors – not checking or not acting on the information

On the test it's often tempting to ostentatiously check the mirrors as frequently as you can when you're driving along a straight bit of road but then end up forgetting when you're doing something more challenging such as tackling a busy junction, which is precisely when you need your mirrors the most. Don't let test nerves distract you from using this vital skill and remember to check your mirrors as your instructor has taught you.

4. Reversing round a corner – ineffective observation or lack of accuracy

Every test requires you to turn your car around and you'll be asked to carry out either this or the turn in the road. Most people find the latter relatively easy (borne out by the fact that it doesn't even make the top ten failures list). But reversing round a corner is a manoeuvre that a lot of people see as their personal bête noire. Getting it right depends on the same principle as the parallel park – thinking things through and not panicking. And remind yourself that you're perfectly capable of doing it successfully; your instructor wouldn't have put you in for your test otherwise.

5. Incorrect use of signals – not cancelling or giving misleading signals

This is another area for potential angst. If you're told to take the next left but put the signal on too early you could be seen as looking as though you're planning to pull into the side of the road. Too late and it might not give other road users enough warning of your intentions. But this is another time to cast off self-doubt. You know you can use the signals correctly, so trust your judgement.

6. Moving away safely – ineffective observations

This manoeuvre can feel quite easy when you're doing it with your instructor, but don't let that make you complacent. Using all your mirrors and remembering to check your blind spot will help ensure you don't fall at this particular fence.

7. Incorrect positioning on the road – at roundabouts or on bends

There's a lot more to positioning your car than keeping it on the right side of the road. Correct positioning means you get the best possible visibility, make your intentions clearer to other road users and allow the traffic to flow freely. It's a sign of a driver who's confident and in control – so show the examiner that's exactly what you are.

8. Lack of steering control – steering too early or leaving it too late

Listening carefully to the directions the examiner gives you and preparing mentally for your next move will help your steering stay smooth. If you don't understand, then ask them to clarify.

9. Incorrect positioning to turn right – at junctions or in one-way streets

Not being in the correct position when you turn right can hold up traffic around you. During your lessons there will have been times when another vehicle turning right will have blocked your way; remembering this and noting how they could have done it differently will help you get it right. Marking the one-way streets on test routes on a map of the area will ensure that you don't end up accidentally treating them like ordinary roads and emerging from them on the wrong side for a right turn.

10. Inappropriate speed – travelling too slowly or being hesitant

Don't make the mistake of thinking that going slowly will impress your examiner and leave them convinced you'll be a responsible driver. They don't want to see you crawling along; they want you to drive at the right speed for the road and traffic conditions. Show them that you can!

Myths about the driving test – fact or fiction?

In the run-up to your test you'll find that well-meaning friends, family, colleagues and old blokes down the pub all want to share 'insider tips' about the driving test. Here's a selection of the most popular. Discover if there's any truth in them.

You should set the mirror slightly off so you have to move your head more and the examiner will see that you're checking regularly.
This advice had a grain of truth in it once, but is now seriously dated. Until 1998 the only mirror in the car would be the usual rear-view mirror, which meant there was more reason for candidates to believe they had to make exaggerated movements to show they were checking properly. However, now it's a requirement for the examiner to also have a traffic mirror, and driving school cars are also often fitted with an eye mirror placed to monitor the student's eye movements. Examiners will also turn as you're driving along and observe you directly, so with different opportunities to observe you there's absolutely no need to go in for 'theatrical looking'. 'Some learners think they have to make exaggerated head movements and bob around like boxers. But it's not about behaving in a way you imagine will impress the examiner,' says driving instructor Malcolm Fortnam. 'The most important thing is to have the mirror in the right place for you – use it effectively and act on what you see.'

You can stall on your test and still pass.
This is true. 'As long as you don't stall in a dangerous situation,

such as on a roundabout, and as long as you handle it properly this needn't count as a major fault and you can still pass your test,' says driving instructor Chris Pope. 'If you stall, correct it, then put it behind you and concentrate on driving as well as you can.'

Examiners have to pass a certain percentage of candidates every week so it's all about quotas, really.

The DSA state that all examiners are trained to carry out the test to the same standard and that they don't have pass or fail quotas. However, every examiner does have to be within 5 per cent of their centre pass rate and 10 per cent of the national pass rate. If this doesn't happen then they are likely to be investigated. And in one instructor's off-the-record opinion, 'This could mean that if an examiner has had a run of good test candidates and given lots of passes, then they might be a bit more critical with the next one because they need to get their average back down. Though, of course, it can also work the other way in that if they've had a run of failures, then they'll be keen to get back on track by passing someone.' But, basically, this is the sort of thing you can't really have any control over so it's best not to worry too much about quotas and concentrate on driving so well they've got no choice but to pass you!

There's this particular examiner at the local test centre who's so grumpy, if you get him then you've no chance of passing.

As mentioned previously, driving examiners have their pass and fail rates screened and they're also checked to make sure they're using all the different test routes and requesting a variety of manoeuvres. So whether they strike you as being grumpy or a total sweetheart, no examiner is really going to be more difficult or easier to get a pass out of than any other.

Driving consultant Kathy Higgins says that seeing your

examiner in a positive light will help you have the right attitude for passing. 'I get on with all the examiners at Garston, which is my local test centre, and tell my students they're great,' says Kathy. 'As it happens it's true, but I'd probably still say it even if there were ones I didn't particularly like. I believe it helps the student relax and feel more upbeat about the coming experience – and that means they're more likely to pass.' So even if you meet your examiner and realise that they do actually fit the description of the Dreaded Grumpy Examiner, don't let it put you off. Remind yourself that prejudice is a Bad Thing and that they're probably a fantastic person really.

That particular test centre is a really difficult one to pass at – the routes are a nightmare.
There are test centres all over the UK and inevitably the road conditions are going to vary a lot. In London you have a high density of traffic, in Cambridge you don't get much opportunity to show off your hill starts and on the Isle of Skye you get a lot of, um, scenery. Every effort is made by the DSA to standardize test routes so that each one contains a mixture of straightforward and more challenging junctions, roundabouts, sections of dual carriageway and so on, but given the nature of our varied land, that's not realistically going to be possible. In the opinion of my off-the-record instructor, 'I think that the way many examiners try to work round this for a more fair result is to accept that in, say, the north of Scotland candidates might not be challenged particularly by the volume of traffic, so they'll demand a rather higher standard in their manoeuvres.' But even taking this into consideration, there are still significant differences in the pass rates of some test centres (see Appendix 2 for full details). The overall pass rate for 2004/5 was 42.3 per cent. However, at the London (Wood Green) centre the pass rate was 26.7 per

cent, in Cambridge (Chesterton Road) it was 51.2 per cent, in Glasgow (Mosspark) it was 29.3 per cent and on the Isle of Skye (Portree) it was 63.6 per cent.

In the opinion of the DSA, the differences aren't just down to quieter or busy road systems. Another factor is that in low-income areas people often have trouble affording lessons and don't have a family car to practise in, so they sometimes come for their test before they're totally prepared and are more likely to fail. However, don't obsess about the pass rates at your local centre. Whether they're low or high it isn't going to make any difference to your particular test; you'll be judged on how you drive on the day and as long as you're at the required standard you'll be fine.

The driving test is so much harder to pass these days, I'm glad I'm not taking my test now.
'Yes, it is,' says Eddie Barnaville, General Manager of the Driving Instructors Association. 'When I was teaching back in the late 1960s it was possible to get most people through in about ten or fifteen lessons. These days that target would be ridiculous. The roads are far busier, which means standards have to be higher. The test has far more components than it used to have – including the reverse parking manoeuvres which many learners struggle with. There's also the "Show me/Tell me" section of the test, and a separate theory test where in the past the candidate would just be asked a few questions on the Highway Code.' Driving instructor Chris Pope agrees, 'It is getting more and more difficult to pass. There's much more traffic on the roads, which creates challenging situations requiring very accurate judgement. Traffic systems have had to become more complex to deal with the volume. For example, a lot of junctions will have several sets of traffic lights rather than just one.'

A National Travel Survey carried out by the DfT in 2005 reports that 'The proportion of young adults holding licences has fallen over the last decade. 42% of women aged 17–20 held a licence in 1992–94 compared to 24% in 2004. The proportions for men were 54% and 29% respectively. This may be due to the car driving test becoming more difficult and/or the introduction of the theory element to the test.' A knock-on effect of the test becoming more difficult is that it takes more lessons to pass, making it a lot more expensive and beyond the financial grasp of many young people. But the fact is there's not a lot you can do about this situation other than learn to drive to the high standard currently required. Alternatively you could try getting your hands on a time machine. Maybe on eBay?

The older you get the more difficult it is to pass your test. And women take much longer than men to pass.

Pass rates for older learners are currently lower than for younger ones. The following figures are from the Car Pass Rates by Age and Gender Survey 2004/5 conducted by the DSA. (For full results, see Appendix 1.)

Pass rates for women

Age	Percentage of successful candidates
17	48.3
20	38.9
30	34.6
40	29.1
50	25.4
60	27.2

Pass rates for men

Age	Percentage of successful candidates
17	51.4
20	45.5
30	40.6
40	37.7
50	32.2
60	31.0

The DfT sample group study of learner drivers, January 2004, showed that women took on average 14.6 months and 2.12 tests to learn and pass, while men took 12 months and 1.87 tests to learn and pass.

To deal with the age issue first, it's clear that those fresh-faced 17-year-old girls knock any later learners out of the water with their impressive overall pass rates. But at the same time, it's clear that plenty of older learners are passing too. The reasons why people often take longer to learn to drive as they get older can vary. Younger people are likely to either still be at college or to have left quite recently, so they're more used to being taught new skills. Driving instructors report that as people get older, they're more likely to question or overanalyse their teaching, whereas younger people just do as they're told, which, if you're dealing with a mechanical device like a car, tends to get the required result. Younger drivers may also feel invincible and not worry about the potential accidents, which means they drive more confidently under supervision and on their tests. However, this quality does mean they're more at risk after passing, when mature drivers tend to be much safer.

However, learning to drive is a very individual process, so if you're an older learner, don't despair. If you've got a natural aptitude you might still learn reasonably quickly and breeze through your test first time. And even if you haven't, you can still be successful, though it may take rather longer. During 2004/5 137 women aged seventy and over passed their test and the oldest woman to pass was ninety-two. Don't see your age as a barrier – they certainly didn't!

As far as the 'men are better at passing their driving tests' issue goes, it's currently true (though maybe you could resolve to help tip the balance on that one by storming to success in your own test). If anyone is ill-mannered enough to have a go at you about that, here are a few useful statistics for your counterattack. Home Office figures for 2003 showed that the following percentages of driving offences were committed by men:

Dangerous driving – 96 per cent
Causing death or bodily harm – 94 per cent
Drink driving – 89 per cent
Speeding – 85 per cent

Women should wear short skirts and low-cut tops, then the examiner will be so busy drooling that he'll pass you.
This is a definite example of flawed logic. If anything, surely the examiner would be more inclined to fail you so you'd have to take your test again and he might get another chance to glimpse your gorgeous cleavage? To say nothing of the fact that you could be examined by a straight woman or a gay man who aren't going to be interested in it anyway. Concentrate on your driving and save your feminine wiles for a time where they're more likely to achieve results, such as getting blokes to buy you drinks in swanky bars.

As your practical test draws closer, you could discover that your new-found confidence in your driving starts to wobble somewhat at the prospect of having to perform under exam conditions. Don't worry though, Chapter 7 will give you plenty of useful strategies to stop nerves from building up beforehand or putting a spanner in the works on your test.

Chapter 7

Your Practical
Test Triumph

Some people feel completely calm at the prospect of taking their practical driving test and are confident they'll breeze through effortlessly. If that's you, then please feel free to skip this chapter, safe in the knowledge that the rest of us are teeth-grittingly envious of you. If, on the other hand, the prospect makes you feel rather anxious, that's perfectly understandable. Exams are nerve-racking at the best of times, and driving tests can feel particularly harrowing. After all, with written exams if you get something wrong you can always go back and cross it out, whereas if you reverse into a bollard on your practical test then your fate is sealed. Knowing that someone is watching and judging your every move can feel pretty bizarre as well. It would be enough to make most people feel bumblingly self-conscious if they were just doing an everyday activity like folding laundry or eating beans on toast, let alone demonstrating a complex skill like driving. Most learners get their knickers in a twist about their test to some extent.

I was very worried about letting my driving instructor down. He was so keen on getting pupils through first time, I was terrified that if I failed he'd feel I'd brought shame on him and all his ancestors and we'd both have to commit hara-kiri together or something. Eva, 33

I was so nervous on my first test I accidentally put my front-door key in the car ignition. It jammed and I couldn't get it out again, so the test had to be cancelled. Jane, 23

I took my test a total of five times before I passed. Two tests I actually took. The three in the middle I got myself in such a state that I refused to leave the test centre building and get into the car. Eventually I got the same examiner twice and he said, 'Look, at least promise me we'll get out of the car park this time.' Amazingly, I passed! Lucy, 24

All these women went on to pass their test and are now capable and confident drivers; so it just goes to show that it can be done! Remember nerves don't mean failure. Most people are nervous. If the only people who passed tests took them in a state of Zen-like calm, there would be very few people on the roads. A degree of nervous tension is actually a good thing; it releases adrenaline, helps you to be extra-alert and on top of your game. But on the other hand, if you get too stressed out that can lead you to make silly mistakes. Basically it's a balancing act, but there are plenty of techniques available to help you get it right. Here's a pick-and-mix selection of strategies you can use in the run-up to your test – ranging from scientifically proven mental and physical calming techniques to spells, crystals and wearing your lucky pants! Choose the ones that appeal to you.

But first, here is the most effective anxiety-reducing advice of all

The absolute, number one, top tip for being less nervous in the run-up to any exam is to be as good as you possibly can be at the skill you're going to be tested on. Do everything you can to get to the highest standard possible before going in to take your test – extra lessons, lots of practice and time spent reading the road as a passenger will all help you raise your game and feel more confident about your test.

Mental strategies

Visualization

Visualization is a technique whereby you repeatedly imagine a positive situation and by doing so help it happen. Your subconscious comes to see this outcome as normal and achievable rather than out of your reach and helps get any emotional blocks out of the way. One of the good things about visualization is that in many ways it's a fancy name for what used to be called 'daydreaming', which means you can do it anywhere – in supermarket queues, on trains and during boring meetings. Here are a few different approaches.

Seeing yourself as a driver – Sometimes people fail their tests because they don't feel they're ready to be a real driver yet. So they self-sabotage by making an out-of-character mistake on their test and failing. If you feel this could be you, it's time to start thinking as though you're already a qualified driver.

- Cut out pictures from magazines of various cars you like the look of and of confident women driving, Then get a photo of yourself and put it at the centre of this driving-heaven collage.

- If your test is in a couple of weeks' time, talk confidently about trips you're planning on making shortly afterwards – 'I'm going to drive over to see Sarah's new flat at the end of the month.'
- Visualize yourself driving. See an image of yourself in your mind's eye bowling along country lanes or parking confidently near your favourite shops. And you're by yourself – no instructor, no mum, dad or boyfriend. You don't need anyone to supervise because you've got your own licence now!

Performing well on your test – Imagine yourself during your driving test, not as a sweaty bag of nerves, but as someone cool, calm and collected. See yourself making good judgements at junctions and roundabouts. Imagine yourself carrying out manoeuvres perfectly. Really tune into the emotions and let yourself savour that sense of satisfaction bordering on smugness that comes from being effortlessly good at something. Finally, let yourself imagine your driving examiner turning to you at the end of your test and telling you that you've passed!

Role-play – If you've got a problem with thinking of yourself as dithery or clumsy, role-play being someone else in your imagination. Would Madonna, Lara Croft, Lady Penelope from *Thunderbirds*, Daisy Duke or Kate Adie be reduced to a quivering wreck by the prospect of her driving test? No, she wouldn't! By temporarily taking on the characteristics of your favourite feisty role model, you can overcome your self-imposed limitations and become more confident in every aspect of your everyday life, not just when it comes to driving.

L

Cognitive behaviour therapy (CBT)

If you've got a tendency towards negative thinking and prophecies of doom (known in CBT as 'catastrophizing'), then using CBT techniques can be really helpful. One approach involves looking at your fears around your test, bringing them down to a more realistic level and replacing them with a more positive viewpoint (called 'reframing'). For example:

I've absolutely got to pass this time. I don't have enough money to carry on with more lessons.
Reframe: Not passing would be a real drag and I'd have to save up again, but I'd still be able to practise in the meantime. And anyway, this is a pointless thing to worry about as my driving is up to standard and I'll probably sail through.

I've absolutely got to be able to drive before I have my baby.
Reframe: It'll be inconvenient if I don't pass this time, but I can have another go shortly afterwards and get through then. It's not the end of the world.

The idea is that you write down whatever your worst fears are about failing and then 'reframe' them in a more down-to-earth way. 'The point of this strategy,' says psychologist Gladeana McMahon, 'is not to make light of your very real concerns about work, money or whatever. Its aim is that by bringing your worries down to a more manageable level and not seeing failure as the end of the world, you'll lessen your anxiety and be more likely to succeed.'

L

Hypnotherapy

Hypnosis is a term derived from the Greek word for sleep and is a technique that can be used to get in touch with your subconscious. Certain suggestions can be made when you're in this receptive state, such as it would be a good idea to stop smoking, or that you can pass your driving test. Booking a personal appointment with a hypnotherapist can be helpful, especially if you feel you've got emotional blocks around driving or have had repeated failures. However, it will cost in the region of £25 to £45 a session and you might need more than one appointment. Also, if you're expecting a dramatic Derren Brown-style experience you may be disappointed – most hypnotherapists only place their clients in a light trance which feels similar to being very relaxed. There are also driving test hypnotherapy CDs available, which take you through a general relaxation session and then a visualization of passing your test. (See 'Reference Section' for details.)

I went to a hypnotherapist and found it worthwhile, though when she was doing that 'counting back from one to ten' thing, I did find it hard not to giggle. Before the actual hypnosis we did a lot of talking about how I felt about driving. My mother never drove and saw it as 'the man's responsibility' and I think I picked up from her that being capable around mechanical things was 'unfeminine'. To be honest, I think the counselling was as useful, if not more so, than the actual hypnosis. It felt great to be able to talk things over with someone who helped me have a fresh take on the situation, especially since, after three failures, I'd exhausted the patience of my family and friends. And I did pass the very next time! Rachel, 40

L

Physical strategies

Breathing exercises

These are great for reducing tension and overcoming panicky feelings. Many people feel the best way to practise breathing exercises is sitting cross-legged in a candlelit room that's been thoroughly feng-shui-ed. If you're in a position to do that, fantastic. But if not, then just having a private space where you can sit or lie down for ten minutes, and maybe close your eyes if you wish, is good enough to be going on with. It can also be helpful to get into the habit of just taking a few minutes when you're in the park or waiting in a queue to tune out other distractions and focus on calming down. Under these circumstances it's fine to keep your eyes open. Like pelvic floor exercises, one of the plus points of breathing exercises is that no one else need know you're doing them.

Here are a couple of different approaches for you to try. Use whatever feels best to you.

Observing your breath
Relax your shoulders, let go of your tensions.
Let your breath out.
Breathe in, slowly and gently.
Breathe out, slowly and gently.
Take just a little longer to breathe out than you did to breathe in.
Focus on letting yourself feel calm and heavy as you breathe out.
Pause and stay empty for a moment.
Breathe in once more.

Gradually the rhythm of your breath will slow down.
Let yourself calmly observe the cycle of your breathing.

I feel calm
Take in a gentle breath. As you breathe out imagine the words, 'I feel calm.' Then imagine each word separately as you breathe out.

> Breathe in gently . . . Breathe out . . . I
> Breathe in gently . . . Breathe out . . . Feel
> Breathe in gently . . . Breathe out . . . Calm

Repeat this sequence getting slower each time. Gradually you will discover that you are leaving longer and longer periods between each word and that it becomes very calming to stay empty for rests before breathing in again.

The major complaint when people start breathing exercises is that it's difficult to stay focused on their breath when other thoughts about work, home or the row they had with their boyfriend keep intruding. This is perfectly normal! Hermits sit in caves on mountainsides for years trying to tune out all distractions through meditation and still end up thinking about what they'll have for breakfast, so you're not alone. The best strategy is to just let the thoughts come and go, without getting too attached to them – just gently draw your attention back to your breathing exercise.

Breathing exercises have been scientifically proven to reduce blood pressure and reduce heart rates. But like going to the gym, you don't necessarily get results immediately. It's good to practise these techniques in advance so you can see their positive effects and by the time your test arrives you'll be able to use them in the waiting room in the test centre and feel confident that they'll work.

Acupressure techniques

Acupressure is like acupuncture, but without the needles. It's based on a form of Chinese medicine which maintains that energy in the body flows along meridians and that putting pressure on certain points along them can assist in staying healthy and stress-free. Two of the points associated with stress are located on the bottom of your middle fingernails, on the side nearest the thumb. Massaging these points with a thumb or fingertip for a few seconds each may help you feel calmer. Give it a go, it's worth a try!

Herbal remedies, Bach Rescue Remedy, aromatherapy

By this point you may be thinking, 'This visualization, breathing and acupressure is all very well, but actually I'd much rather just go to the doctor and get "something for my nerves".' Don't, though. For a start, the days when GPs used to hand out tranquillizer prescriptions to all comers are long gone, so you'd probably end up hanging round their waiting room reading three-year-old back copies of *My Weekly* for nothing. Second, life is full of stressful situations and it's best to get into the habit of coping with them via methods other than medication. And third, many tranquillizers can affect your reflexes, and would be likely to bring down your performance on your test anyway. Here are some better options:

Herbal tablets – Tablets such as Kalms can be helpful in soothing your nerves without having the negative side-effects of prescription drugs. They need to be taken for a week before your test and can be purchased from all good chemists.

Bach flower remedies – You may have already been using Bach flower remedies to help you with anxieties about your lessons. But even if you haven't you still might like to take Rescue Remedy in the run-up to your test. This is a combination of five of the flower essences devised to help in stressful situations and is available from most health food shops.

I knocked back Rescue Remedy on the day of my test and found it really calmed me down. I don't think I'd have passed without it. Abigail, 27

Aromatherapy – Aromatherapy involves using essential oils from various plants and can be used to treat a wide range of health problems, including stress. Three of the best for anxiety are geranium, lavender and basil. Adding between five and ten drops of the oil to a bath once it has been run or putting a few drops on a handkerchief and inhaling them can be very soothing.

Spiritual and New Age techniques and good luck charms

Crystals – Some people believe crystals can have healing and magical qualities and that they work like lenses, focusing electromagnetic energy to help balance body and mind. You can buy them relatively cheaply at new age shops. Bloodstone will make you more assertive if your driving problem is hesitancy and ˙rose quartz is good if your problem is being too hard on yourself. If you've a tendency towards road rage, amethyst will calm you down, while tiger's eye – linked to integrating brain hemispheres – is good for those pesky reversing manoeuvres. Keep your crystal near by you, perhaps on your desk or bedside table, so you can absorb its energies. Some crystals, such as amethyst, are often made into jewellery, so maybe you could choose one that's set in a ring or necklace. A smaller crystal can be carried round in your pocket, that way it can even get to help you during your driving lessons and test.

Good luck charms – Such as a four-leaf-clover-symbol, or a pebble that's had a hole worn all the way through it. Not a rabbit's foot though, that's just nasty.

Wearing your lucky pants – That always works!

The big day

By the evening before your test, your instructor will have taught you all he can and believe you're ready to pass. You are ready to pass. All you need to do is believe in yourself and by this time tomorrow you'll be the proud owner of your very own driving licence! All the time, money and stress will have been worth it.

Things to do the night before

It's important to lay out the documents you'll need in advance. Your test can't be conducted without the correct paperwork and apparently a surprising number of people turn up without it. Then get your outfit sorted, especially if you're prone to 'Oh

God, everything is in the wash and I've got nothing to wear' wardrobe crises. Racing around fretting about laddered tights or a broken zip on your skirt won't be the best way to start the day. Casual clothes are best and layers can be a good idea. Nerves can have you alternating between feeling cold with terror and hot and flustered, so it's a good idea to be able to respond to whatever your emotional thermostat is doing. When it comes to shoes, the ones you've worn for most of your lessons are the best bet. Don't forget your glasses/contact lenses, or sunglasses if the weather might be bright. It's best to have your hair tied back in order for the examiner to have a clear view of your eye movements, so if you've got long hair or a fringe find a suitable hairband, hairclip or (if you must) scrunchie. You might also want to find a book or magazine to read in the waiting room in case you need something to distract you. Then get your Bach Rescue Remedy/aromatherapy oils/good luck charm of choice to hand as well and you're completely prepared for the challenges of the following day!

Now it's time to relax, or at least distract yourself from any build-up of nerves. Taking some exercise would be a great idea – maybe swimming, a dance class or the gym. It'll release upbeat endorphins and remind you how powerful and capable you really are. If you go out with friends make it an early night and avoid alcohol. You don't want to wake up groggy, and if you have a morning test it could still be in your bloodstream and affect your performance the next day. It's probably best to avoid your test as a topic of conversation too. You don't want to risk either having to sit through your mates' driving-test horror stories or being on the receiving end of so much pink and fluffy love and encouragement that you become extra-paranoid about letting them down by failing.

If you spend the evening at home, a good way of distracting yourself is to have a decluttering session. Sort out your wardrobe, make-up bag, work or college files. It's a very absorbing pastime and will leave you with a real sense of achievement. Or you could curl up and watch a movie. Ideally an inspirational one with a positive role model of a woman learning a skill and triumphing against the odds. For example: *Bend it Like Beckham*, *Erin Brockovich*, *Working Girl*, *My Fair Lady*, *Private Benjamin*, *Little Voice* or *Strictly Ballroom*.

Listening to soothing music in a hot bath, drinking hot milk or camomile tea and having an early night would be a good way to round the evening off. If you have trouble sleeping, don't worry. Although prolonged sleep deprivation can have a negative effect on performance, one broken night won't do you any harm. Do some of your visualizations and drift off imagining yourself enjoying the freedom and confidence of driving anywhere you like on your own.

The day itself

When you wake up, you may find you're suffering from 'school pain'. That 'queasy and headachy combined with strange palpitations' feeling that so often afflicts us when we've got something lined up that we'd rather duck out of. Getting your mum to write you a sick note so that you can spend the day on the sofa watching telly and drinking Heinz tomato soup isn't an option this time though. The best way to deal with feelings like this is not to ignore them, but not to engage with them too much either – just see them as a minor annoyance, like flies at a picnic.

If you're on a diet, give yourself the day off. It's important that you're able to concentrate properly and not be distracted by feeling 'spacey' or a rumbling tum. Ideally have a good breakfast, but even if you feel too nervous to eat, try to get something down you, if only a piece of toast or a banana.

If you have to go into work or college beforehand, throw yourself into it. Steaming through your to-do list or pitching in with your opinions in seminars will give you a sense of achievement, impress your boss or tutors – and stop you dwelling on your test.

It's usual to have a practice lesson with your instructor before the practical test, as a sort of warm-up gig to get you feeling comfortable behind the wheel. Don't worry if you make mistakes during this session; remember that a bad dress rehearsal often means a great performance.

Forget the idea of being fashionably late for your test. Test centres run to a very tight schedule and if you don't turn up on time then no amount of batting your eyelashes and apologizing prettily will make them relent. You're just going to have to book and pay for another one, princess.

The waiting room

So, you and your instructor have arrived in plenty of time. Well done! Sitting in the waiting room with the other candidates and their instructors tends be a tad nerve-racking and you'll probably feel as if the tension-dial is being turned up unbearably. If you've brought a magazine, book or iPod get it out to distract yourself. This is also a good time to get your deep-breathing or acupressure exercises going. And remember you're not alone – all the other examinees will be feeling just as wobbly on the inside. Then all the examiners troop in. The one allocated to you will call out your name and introduce themselves. There's a brief flurry of sorting out paperwork – and you're off!

Top tips for passing your test

- Remember the lessons you've had that have gone well – the times you've driven confidently in heavy traffic or executed a manoeuvre perfectly and been praised by your instructor. Remind yourself that your instructor wouldn't be putting you in if he didn't think you were good enough. You deserve to pass this test!

- If you start off feeling a shaky, sweaty-palmed bag of nerves, don't panic. It won't be this bad for the whole of the test. You'll find that after a few minutes you'll settle down into your driving and be giving your attention to the road rather than your emotional state and your symptoms will ease off.

- If the thought of being tested freaks you out, stop thinking of it as a test. Instead, imagine that you're just taking someone home and as you don't know where they live they have to give you directions.

- When you're asked to do manoeuvres, you can pretend this person doesn't know how to drive and wants you to show them a few of the basics.

- If you've got a supervising examiner sitting in with you, don't worry about them. They'll be assessing your examiner, not you. In fact, it can make the situation feel easier in that you're not the only one being examined – the person sitting next to you is in the same boat!

- Most people have a 'least favourite' manoeuvre which they'll be hoping and praying the examiner doesn't choose. But don't waste energy trying to channel powerful thought-vibes in an attempt to influence their decision, because it's not going to work.

- If you don't understand what the examiner has asked

you to do, don't be afraid to ask them to repeat themselves.

- The examiner might chat during the test to help put you at your ease. If you find this helpful, great. If not, just say that you find talking distracting. Alternatively, just give brief answers and they'll soon get the message. And don't worry, they won't be offended. Their aim is to help you be as relaxed as possible so you can focus on your driving.

- If you feel you're messing up a manoeuvre, just pull forwards and do it again correctly. As long as you haven't done anything wrong such as touched the kerb or failed to make good observations you can still pass.

- If you feel you've made a mistake, don't instantly assume you've failed – it might only have been a minor fault. Put it behind you and carry on driving as well as you can. And restrain yourself from sighing or muttering foul curses under your breath; the last thing you want to do is draw attention to your little lapse.

- Don't freak out if you run into bad or unexpected conditions. Going down a narrow one-way street to find a bin lorry reversing into it, an emergency vehicle behind you and a crocodile of schoolchildren appearing from nowhere can feel like a lot to deal with at the time. But avoid the temptation to burst into tears or go aaargh! See it as an opportunity to show that you can deal confidently with all situations.

- Even if it's very clear that you've made a major fault and failed, don't let yourself go to pieces. Carry on driving as well as you can and aim to keep your faults down. After all, the fewer faults you have the more confident you'll feel when it comes to taking your test again.

- Tempting as it may be, don't try to eyeball what the examiner is writing or work out if their little marks mean you've passed or failed. Keep your attention on the road!

Pass or fail? The verdict

By the time you're back at the test centre you may have an idea about whether you've passed or failed, or you might not have a clue. The examiner will get you to turn the engine off, complete their paperwork and then say one of two things.

I'm pleased to tell you that you have reached the standard required.
That's fantastic! Well done! The examiner will probably still want to give you some feedback about how you performed on the test and offer advice on how you can improve. Don't worry if you don't take it all in, your instructor can recap on the drive home and you can talk about whether you should take a motorway lesson or Pass Plus course then too. Now you can proceed directly to Chapter 9, 'You've Passed: Losing Your L-Plates'!

I am sorry to say that you have not reached the standard required at this time.
Oh, that's horrible and so disappointing! But it's not the end of the world. Go to Chapter 8, 'If at First You Don't Succeed', for advice that will help you bounce back and make sure it's your turn next time.

Chapter 8

If at First You Don't Succeed

Oh no! You were hoping you'd pass your practical test first time and wouldn't have to bother with this section, weren't you? But it's OK. It really is going to be OK. Remember, according to a 2004 DfT sample study of learner drivers, the average amount of times it takes for women to pass is 2.1. So although you're naturally disappointed that you're not going to be breaking open the champagne tonight, your situation is perfectly normal. See it as a postponement, not a cancellation. Your day will soon come! But in the meantime you're going to have to get through the present one.

Presumably, by the time you're reading this you'll have survived the Drive of Shame with your instructor back to your home, college or workplace. You'll probably have been upset or embarrassed and might even have got a bit tearful. But don't worry, it won't have been anything they won't have seen many times before. And hopefully your instructor will have been sympathetic and positive about the future. 'I think it's really important how you work with students on the drive back from a failed test,' says driving instructor Liz Mitchell. 'I don't bother with in-depth analysis then. Often students can't remember much as they're too upset. Initially I focus on comforting them – we can analyse what went wrong and make plans to put it right at the next lesson.'

L

First aid for your feelings

The chances are you feel dreadful right now and in desperate need of first aid for your mangled emotions. Here are some suggestions to help soothe your bruised ego and generally put you back on your feet.

- Have a good cry. If your driving instructor has taken you straight home, then this is an excellent opportunity to crawl under the duvet and bawl your eyes out. It's tremendously therapeutic.
- Call or email your mum. Mums tend to be brilliant in this sort of situation. Also contact any friends who you know are going to say all the right things. These include, 'I failed first time myself, you'll get through next, no worries', 'People who pass second time make better drivers anyway' and 'Let's meet up tonight and do something nice to take your mind off it.'
- Take your dog for a walk or curl up with your cat. They love you unconditionally and couldn't care less whether you've passed your test or not.
- Put some bouncy, uplifting music on.
- At the first opportunity, give yourself a treat. You might not have passed your test today, but it's important to be rewarded not just for success but for effort, for being brave enough to try. Buy yourself a bunch of flowers or splash out on a book or nail varnish to cheer yourself up. Avoid major.purchases though – mangled emotions can often throw a glitch into your style radar and you could end up with an expensive mistake.
- Forget about the things you 'ought' to do such as laundry

or going to the gym and do something fun such as watching a DVD or going clubbing with your friends.

- If you've had to go back to work or college, confide in your friends but avoid anyone who might sneer or make jokes at your expense. If you can't avoid the company of such an unpleasant individual (they're your boss, for example), be brisk and matter of fact about the situation and get stuck into whatever type of work keeps contact with them to a minimum.

- If you're feeling wobbly and upset, spend your time on low-key tasks such as dealing with paperwork and allow yourself to put off challenging stuff such as calling that difficult client until another day.

- Although having a good cry is great, if you're at work or college the logistics can be a bit tricky, what with the girl in the next cubicle getting to hear and you ending up with streaked mascara and blotchy face. So if possible put that on hold until you get back home – by which time you'll probably feel better anyway.

- Try to take a coffee break or early lunch at the earliest opportunity. It'll give you a chance to make some calls or just relax with a magazine or book.

- And don't worry that failing means you'll make a bad driver in the future. 'Whether or not you pass first time doesn't have any relevance to what sort of driver you'll become in the long term,' says driving consultant Kathy Higgins. 'It took me three attempts to get my licence, but now I've got every advanced driving qualification going and also train driving instructors!'

In the course of the day following your driving test make notes on anything you can remember about it: the route you took, the faults you made and where you made them and your emotional state. Otherwise you might forget this information before your next lesson and it'll be really helpful to you and your instructor for planning how to overcome any problems and be successful next time.

The morning after

For most people the emotional impact of failing their test is painful in the short term, but like a stubbed toe it passes quickly. By the following day you'll probably have regained your equilibrium and be feeling hopeful about your next test. However, others continue to have issues about their test. Here are a selection of possible reactions and suggestions on how to deal with them.

I was robbed!
According to the DSA's annual report for 2004/5, 87 per cent of candidates said they felt their test result was fair. If you're one of the ones who didn't, it's still sensible to accept the result with good grace rather than get all bitter and twisted or do something undignified like rant at the examiner and generally carry on like someone out of a Jerry Springer show. Anyone who assaults an examiner will not only have the usual charges pressed but also has to pay a double test fee to cover the cost of a second examiner to provide extra security on their next test!

If you are determined to appeal, you've got six months to do it if you live in England and Wales, twenty-one days if you live in Scotland. However, it's worth bearing in mind that even if the appeal goes in your favour, you can't have the examiner's decision reversed. The best you can hope for is an outside chance of claiming the moral high ground and having your driving test fee refunded. Is that really going to be worth all the hassle? It's much wiser to accept that you failed because your driving wasn't up to scratch. And remember that even though you might feel put out by the result at the moment, your failed test may well have saved your life. It's proved you're not ready to be out on your own yet and has made sure you get the extra tuition you need.

I've let everyone down.
After a failed test it's tempting to wallow in extravagant self-reproach of the 'I've let myself down, I've let my driving instructor down, I've let my parents down' variety. 'Pupils can come under a lot of pressure from their peer group and their families,' says driving instructor Liz Mitchell. 'They're worried about everyone else's reaction and their own needs and feelings often come at the bottom of the list.' It can be hard if your partner is disappointed because you still can't share the driving, or if your lessons are going to cost your parents even more cash. But the fact is you did your best and no one can ask for more than that.

Right, that's it, I'm giving up!
People take failure in different ways. Some find it so devastating for their self-esteem that they get into an 'I'm a worthless, useless muppet' mind-set that can be quite difficult to clamber back out of. But you're not! No, really you're not! You are a wonderful person deserving of love, happiness, all the good things life has to offer (and that includes a driving licence). Another common attitude is the 'If I can't win, I won't play' approach – this is especially likely if success has always come fairly easily in other areas, such as school or work. But if you

and your instructor both know you're ready and this failure is just a blip, then this is a time to control your emotions rather than let them control you. If you really want that licence you'll just have to knuckle down, sign up for more lessons, take another test. You know the drill.

I can't afford any more lessons or test fees.
Unlike the other attitudes, which can be sorted out with the right emotional support, financial concerns need to be addressed sensibly. There's no doubt that learning to drive is an expensive business, and if the money isn't there, it just isn't. However, it's worth bearing in mind that if you're at test standard giving up now will mean that your skills go off the boil and it'll cost you more in the long run to get them back up again. If there are other areas, such as socializing, that you can cut back on, or if it's possible for you to raise more cash through overtime, then it's a good idea to just grit your teeth and do it. And if that's not possible, then at least try to keep your skills ticking over by getting in as much driving practice as you can.

Booking your next test

Unless something has gone wildly wrong, it's common practice for instructors to suggest retaking your test as soon as you possibly can. After all, they wouldn't have put you in for your first test if they didn't think you were ready.

The first date you're allowed to retake your test is ten working days after the last one. This is so you'll have time to have a couple of top-up lessons to tidy up your skills. However, the average waiting time for practical tests is currently between six to eight weeks, so your instructor will probably suggest you call up or go online to try to get a cancellation.

Unlike your first test, which you probably booked well in advance, and at a time when you and your instructor could compare your diaries, a certain amount of ducking and diving can be required to get a cancellation at a time that's convenient for you both. Ask your driving instructor to give you some available slots and then get in touch with the DSA to rebook. You might have to call several times before you get lucky, but be persistent until a suitable cancellation comes up. When you've got a test booked, call and inform your instructor. He'll want to know as soon as possible so he can book lessons into the remaining free time.

Post-match analysis – where did it all go wrong?

If this is your first or second failure, chances are there's no great need for anguished soul-searching or a major overhaul of your game plan. Probably all that's required is to polish up your skills a bit and sort out any problems with your nerves, which are almost certainly going to be better second time round anyway. However, on your next lesson it's important to analyse the test with your instructor. The examiner will have given you a driving test report showing the faults marked during the test. Unless you failed through having more than fifteen driving (formerly 'minor') faults, the major faults are the ones you'll both need to focus on. Talk to your instructor about what you can remember about the test. It'll all help him form a picture of how the test went and what needs to be improved for you to succeed.

What type of faults?

If you've always had trouble with parking or roundabouts, you'll probably have embarked on your test worried that this would be your particular downfall. And, indeed, you may have been right. But not necessarily. People are often stunned by failing their test on an aspect of driving they usually handle really well. What's that all about?

I failed my first test on just one fault – because I stopped over the stop line at some traffic lights. I'm a naturally cautious driver and had never done that before in all my lessons. Hesitancy had always been my problem and I thought that if I failed on anything it would be that. Bizarre. Siobhan, 29

Basically, it's about the fact that driving tests aren't an exact science and that stress can do strange things to people. Driving instructor Chris Pope says, 'If a student sees a particular aspect of driving as their "weak area" they can become so preoccupied by it that it affects their ability to concentrate on other areas. However, to be a safe and capable driver, it's important to be rounded and confident with all aspects of driving – so failure will be a sign that you just weren't ready to pass at that point.'

In between now and your next test, it's a good idea to practise any aspects of driving you had problems with. Driving consultant Kathy Higgins also recommends 'returning to the scene of the crime'. 'I always take my pupils back to the places where the mistakes took place, so they have the opportunity to carry out the manoeuvre or negotiate that particular junction successfully – it proves to them they can do it.'

How many faults were there?

If you only had one or two major faults then that's a lot easier to deal with psychologically. The failed test can be reframed as a 'near miss' and you can feel confident that with a bit more tuition and a more relaxed approach, you'll get through next time. However, if you had a large number of faults or committed a dangerous fault, then you'll both want to talk over what went wrong in greater depth. It might have just been down to nerves, but then again, it could be a sign that you shouldn't go back for your test straight away but instead take another block of lessons to improve your skills.

Was it just nerves?

It's entirely possible that your failure was mainly down to nervousness under test conditions, leading you to make mistakes you wouldn't have made under normal circumstances. If you suspect that's the case, then you can feel especially optimistic. Have a look at Chapter 7 for some tips on calming your nerves. However, you'll probably find the mere fact that it's now a known quantity makes a huge difference.

L

Inspiring cheesy quotations

When your confidence has been knocked, cheesy quotations can often prove a surprising source of strength. The best ones are those that you come across yourself and somehow strike a chord with you personally. But here are a few to be going on with:

'Success is about how high you bounce when you hit bottom.' George Patton

'When I thought I couldn't go on, I forced myself to keep going. My success is based on persistence, not luck.' Estee Lauder

'Many of life's failures are people who did not realize how close they were to success when they gave up.' Thomas Edison

'Courage is going from failure to failure without losing enthusiasm.' Winston Churchill

'I've always lived by the creed that you're never a failure in life when you fall as long as you get up again.' Evel Knievel

'Life shrinks or expands in proportion to one's courage.' Anaïs Nin

Your second test

Most learners report feeling far more relaxed and positive about their test the second time around. It's like the curtain of terror has been ripped aside and – hey, it's only a driving test. However, if your first test was particularly stressful – maybe you got a lot of faults or you felt uncomfortable with your driving examiner – you could be feeling even more wound up. But remind yourself this is a different situation, a different day, and you'll probably get a different examiner too. And bear in mind the quote, 'Today's opportunities erase yesterday's failures.'

Next time round I went into it feeling I had a fairly good chance. By then I realized there was a lot of luck involved in terms of what the traffic was like on the day and so I was more philosophical. I also felt pretty sure that even if something took me by surprise I wouldn't fall apart and do anything dangerous. Passed second time. Narinder, 20

As God is my witness, I will pass my driving test! Overcoming multiple failures en route to success

OK, so you've failed once, twice . . . and it wasn't third time lucky either. And it's reaching the point where you're having trouble staying optimistic. What if you're jinxed and cursed and doomed where driving is concerned? What if you're destined to spend all your disposable income on more and more lessons and test fees, only to end up in the *Guinness Book of Records* as the woman to have failed the most driving tests ever? Maybe you should just accept that some people aren't destined to be drivers and give up? During dark nights of the soul like this it can be hard to keep believing in yourself. But this is exactly the time when you need to draw on your inner reserves. Getting your driving licence might be a battle, but it's one worth fighting. And doing so will strengthen your character and make you better able to cope with problems in the future. After all, if there's one thing that unites high achievers from Marie Curie to Nicole Kidman, it's the ability to bounce back from failure.

So let's look at this from the 'It's not failure, it's a learning experience' angle. What exactly are you learning from your unsuccessful tests? Well, first, it's that your current approach isn't working. Your driving skills, your nerves or maybe both are letting you down. It's time for a bit of detective work to find out what's at the root of the problem.

Driving-related reasons

Maybe you've been put in for your test too early –
Although most instructors are good judges of when their pupils are ready to go for their test and won't put you in before you're ready, some do get it wrong. This might be because their judgement is lacking. Or they could have an unprofessional attitude and are hoping to off-load you for reasons of their own. Maybe they've got a waiting list and want to bump you off so they can take on new students. Maybe you're always late for lessons and that gets on their

nerves. But whatever their motivation might be there is no justification for putting you in for your test too early. To find out if this might be the case, book a lesson with another instructor, explain the situation and ask if they feel that you're ready for your test. Being with an unfamiliar person in an unfamiliar car might mean you don't drive quite to your usual standard during this session, but if, even taking this into account, they still feel you're not up to the required level then it's probably time to change to an instructor who'll be straight with you and continue your lessons with them.

Maybe you should consider a new instructor – This is a very personal thing; some pupils feel very loyal to their instructors and are sure that any problems are down to themselves. If that's the case for you and you're sure your loyalty isn't misguided, then don't split up at this point.

If, however, you've always felt a bit uncomfortable with your instructor – perhaps found them overcritical or had trouble understanding their explanations when they were talking to you about something you were struggling with – then perhaps it's time to move on. You could have just got into a rut together, where they've reached the limit of what they're able to teach you and a fresh approach could be just what you need. If you decide to take the plunge, see the tips on changing your instructor on pp. 43–5.

Or maybe a change from a manual to an automatic car might do the trick – If you've got almost to the point of passing with a manual car then it's probably worth sticking with it. The advantage of passing your test on a manual is that you'll be qualified to drive both a manual and an automatic car, whereas if you pass on an automatic that's all you're allowed to drive. However, many struggling learners do rave about how much easier it is to handle an automatic car, so this could potentially be the key to turning things around.

I'd had a couple of dismal failures on a manual car and was on the verge of giving up hope that I'd ever have a driving licence when I decided to try an automatic. It was so much easier! I'd never felt confident about clutch control and with only the brake and accelerator to deal with I was able to give so much more attention to the road and what was happening around me. My observations (always a problem) improved tremendously and when I took my automatic test I passed first time. Debbie, 42

Psychological reasons

If you're a capable driver when you're out with your instructor but repeatedly go to pieces on your driving test, it's likely that there are deeper issues at stake than run-of-the mill driving-test nerves. So a certain amount of digging away in the murky depths of your psyche might be helpful.

Do you have issues about exams and being tested? – If you've got a history of finding exam situations particularly stressful, then you're likely to find your driving test difficult too. And even if you've always felt fairly confident about written exams and have tended to do well in them, your driving test can feel like a different kettle of fish altogether, especially if it's a skill you've struggled with. This could be one of the rare times – or maybe even the first – that you've had to face failure. And because that's an unknown quantity it can feel especially scary.

So what's the best way to handle the situation? If you're at college and finding exam situations are a problem for you, then seeing a student counsellor could help by giving you the opportunity to talk over why you find them so stressful. You can then find an approach to dealing with exams that's suited to you as an individual. It might also be valuable to see a counsellor if you feel your failed tests are linked to problems you have with self-esteem in your everyday life.

Another approach – and as far as your long-term driving future is concerned an even better one – is to get your skills to a very high level. 'Some people do find the stress of being tested really gets to them,' says driving consultant Kathy Higgins. 'So I aim to get them driving at a level that's well above the required standard. That way, even if their performance is affected by nerves they can still pass.'

Are you afraid of driving alone? – Anecdotal evidence indicates that a significant number of women drivers never get behind the wheel after passing their tests because of lack of confidence. And maybe you could be unconsciously sabotaging yourself when it comes to your driving test because you know that once you've passed you'll be out there on your own – and you don't feel ready for that yet! Even if you're at the stage where you're able to steel yourself to deal capably with busy junctions or dual carriageways, if deep down you're terrified of them then failure could be your way of ensuring that you don't have to deal with them without backup. If you think that might be the case, talk it over with your driving instructor. If you're able to appear outwardly cool and competent, he'll probably have no idea of your inner turmoil. Maybe it would be a good idea to forget about the test for a while and concentrate on building up your confidence. Alternatively, going to a hypnotherapist or trying visualization could help.

After my third failed test I was running out of money and was on the verge of giving up. It was so frustrating – my driving instructor knew I could do it and so did I. Deep down I think I was scared of having to drive alone and so that's why I kept failing – it was my subconscious blocking me. In desperation I tried some visualization techniques where I imagined myself driving alone through beautiful countryside, feeling relaxed and happy. I passed the very next time and I reckon that was what did the trick. Rose, 29

Taking a break

If you're close to passing your test it's generally better to keep trying rather than to give up at this point. Stopping lessons can mean you'll lose your momentum and your skills will become rusty. However, for some people taking a break will be the right decision. In much the same way that it can be good to forget about slimming after a period of yo-yo dieting, or to commit to staying single for a while after a series of useless boyfriends, putting driving on the back-burner for a bit is a perfectly valid option if you're feeling seriously demoralized by it and locked into a sort of 'repetitive failure syndrome'. Taking a break – whether that's a few months, a year or even longer – often means that when you do go back to it you'll be in a different frame of mind to the one you're in at the moment, maybe with fewer pressures in other areas of your life and a greater maturity and confidence.

Recognizing whether or not it's the right time to learn is important. I took lessons at seventeen but I found them really stressful. I already had A levels, a Saturday job, a busy social life and my first serious boyfriend to cope with and driving just felt like another pressure – when my driving instructor rang on the doorbell I used to feel sick! I failed twice then gave up just before my exams. Secretly I felt relieved to have an excuse. I had another go when I was job-hunting after uni and found it loads easier; life was less frantic and I felt more able to cope with the ups and downs of driving. Emma, 23

Keeping the faith

As the failed tests mount up, it can be difficult to stay optimistic. But it's important not to be dragged down. Avoid moaning endlessly to your family and mates, or saying things like, 'I'm so useless, I'll never pass.' 'We tend to get what we focus on,' says driving instructor Liz Mitchell. 'If you focus on failure, you're more likely to repeat it. Instead, think about how fantastic it will be when you have your driving licence – the freedom it will bring and how proud of yourself you'll feel.' And ultimately success will be yours. Many people who've had multiple failures experience it like some mysterious shift that comes from nowhere.

I passed on my fourth attempt. I was in the middle of the test and it was like everything just fell into place. I felt really confident driving along and it was like 'This is so stupid, what was my problem beforehand?' It was my head that was stopping me, even though I could do it. Rachel, 40

Success always feels brilliant, but there's something about success you've had to fight for which makes it extra special. You've confronted something that you found really difficult and triumphed. You've shown grit, determination, and believed in yourself when the chips were down. You are the heroine of your own life. You're a star!

I took loads of lessons and five tests to pass. My family and friends started to get a bit embarrassed and stopped asking how I was doing. I'm sure they all thought I should just jack it in. But there was always this stubborn part of me that refused to be defeated. Sort of like Scarlett O'Hara raising her fist to heaven – 'As God is my witness, I'll never wait at the bus stop in the rain again.' Naomi, 34

Whether you pass second time, seventh or seventeenth, you deserve your licence every bit as much as someone who breezed through on their very first test. And you'll probably value and appreciate it even more. The next chapter, 'You've Passed: Losing Your L-Plates', will guide you through your first drives, provide advice on safety and help you make the most of the freedom and independence that comes with finally being a qualified driver.

Chapter 9

You've Passed: Losing Your L-Plates

'You've passed' – hearing those magic words from your examiner is a very special moment in anyone's life.

Oh my God, it was amazing. After years of struggling I couldn't believe I'd finally done it and was now a proper, qualified driver just like my friends. I felt as if I'd been lifted up to a higher plane of human existence or something. Naomi, 34

Your driving examiner will give you a copy of the driving test report and even though you've passed he might still want to talk to you about any minor faults you've made and point out a few ways you could improve your driving. Do your best to listen to his advice, though it's likely you'll be in such a daze you won't be able to take it in. Call your instructor over so that they can listen in and will be able to recap if you go on to take a motorway lesson or Pass Plus course with them. The examiner will also give you a pass certificate.

The examiner will offer to take your provisional licence and arrange for a full licence to be sent to you. However, if your provisional licence was issued before 1 March 2004, it's a foreign licence or you've since changed your name (for example, through marriage) that won't be possible and you'll have to complete the paperwork and send it off to DVLA yourself. If you're taking the latter option – beware! If you don't do it within two years then your test pass certificate becomes invalid and you'll be required to retake your theory and practical tests again – nightmare!

You should be sent your full licence within three weeks, but are legally allowed to drive in the meantime, so long as you haven't developed a medical condition that would prevent you. Even though you've passed, your instructor or a friend should drive you home as you'll probably be too hyped-up to be safe on the road. Realizing that the slog and expense of lessons is behind you and that you're now a real driver is a wonderful thing, so savour your triumph!

- Text and email all your family and friends and enjoy their congratulations bouncing back at you.
- Have a ceremonial tearing up of the L-plates and get someone to take a photo of you doing it for posterity.
- Have a night out to celebrate – and book a taxi home, so you can have a drink if you want. This isn't the time to be brought down to earth by the responsibilities that go with being a driver.

Really learning to drive

Once you finished celebrating, your new life as a driver can begin! However, you'll notice that one of the rather annoying things people will do is to adopt a knowing demeanour and say, 'Ah, it's only once you've passed your test that you really learn to drive.' As if the blood, sweat and tears of your lessons and the fiery baptism of your driving test counted for nothing. But don't let your pride be bruised. What they're actually trying to say, via this rather cryptic pronouncement, is that although you've acquired the basic skills to stay safe on the road, in the future you're going to face lots of new driving situations, some that you'll breeze through and others you'll find more challenging. You'll learn what it is to drive at night, go on long journeys, find parking spots in busy cities, get lost and then find your way again, drive in bad weather conditions, drive when you're tired or upset, drive with children in the back, deal with other people's road rage (and learn to suppress any of your own), get stuck in a five-mile tailback and so on and on.

Every new experience you deal with successfully will help make you a better driver in the long term. But until you've built that experience up, you will be at greater risk of having an accident. A 2005 report by the Association of British Insurers (ABI) states that new drivers are more likely to have an accident in the first two years after passing their test than at any other time in their driving career. So it's important to see yourself as being at the beginning of a learning curve. You'll need to decide whether you want to take a Pass Plus course, wear P-plates on your car – and when to take your very first drive alone!

Pass Plus

One of the best things you can do for yourself as a new driver is to take a Pass Plus course. This is a series of one-hour modules covering areas of driving such as night, motorway and country driving. It'll give you the opportunity to experience types of driving you might not have been able to cover in your lessons. There isn't a test at the end, but you are assessed by the instructor to ensure you've reached the required standard. Normally it takes about six hours, though for some people it can take a little longer, and modules can be taken separately or in one long session. The latter can be useful in that it'll give you the opportunity to drive in different terrain – city girls have the chance to deal with narrow rural lanes and country ones will be able to travel to a big city and tackle urban driving. Driving instructor Clive Greenaway, who is based in Bournemouth, says, 'I take my students through the Dorset countryside up to London, round Hyde Park Corner and back again. On the way up I guide the student, and then get them to take full responsibility on the way back.'

The course costs about £150, but many car insurers give significant discounts to new drivers who take it, so it can often pay for itself, and sometimes will save you extra on top of that.

However, despite the benefits of the Pass Plus course, only about 18 per cent of newly qualified drivers actually take it. Chris Marquis at the AA feels that this is often because, 'Once they've passed, many ex-pupils have an attitude of "I know it all now, there's nothing more you can teach me." Others do realize they'd benefit from extra tuition, but just can't face any more lessons and are desperate to see the back of their instructor.'

Another reason for avoiding the course might be that you feel you've 'got away with it' in passing your test and are worried about driving again with your old or a new instructor who might look at your driving and think, 'Hold on a minute, this girl should never have passed.' But don't worry about it, you got your licence because you deserve it, and even if you're a bit nervous or rusty on your Pass Plus course, your instructor will help you make the most of it and reach the required standard.

So do take the Pass Plus course if you possibly can. It'll be an investment in safe driving for your future. And you might actually be surprised to find you like it.

I enjoyed my Pass Plus course. I was still on a high from having passed my test and it felt good to go out with my instructor feeling as though we were equals. I found the motorway driving particularly useful as he got

*me to practise coming off and joining them over and over, pushing me in
a way my partner just wouldn't have.* Lucy, 24

From L-plates to P-plates?

Displaying P (provisional driver) plates on your car is advisable
during your first year of driving. Many new drivers don't want
to as they see them as being a bit embarrassing. But they will
help you stay safe and avoid accidents because other drivers
will realize you're inexperienced and give you more leeway.
As Chris Marquis at the AA says, 'They can take the heat out
of the situation. If other drivers see you make a mistake or
being hesitant they spot the plates and realize it's because
you're a novice rather than thinking you're a twit.'

Your very, very first drive alone

You could be nervous at the prospect of your first drive alone,
or you could be straining at the leash. Either way, the experience tends to be both surreal and exhilarating. Surreal because
you're on your own for the first time ever, and exhilarating for
the same reason. This is the moment when it tends to sink in
that you've really, really done it. You've passed!

Before setting off inform your insurance company that
you've passed and check that you know how to operate all the
car controls. You'll need to be able to give all your attention to
the road rather than fiddling around trying to work out which
is the indicator and which is the windscreen wipers. You should
fit P-plates as well – even if you don't want to display them for
a whole year, you could just use them for the first month.

It's best to keep your first drive short and easy to build up your confidence – maybe following a route that you've done frequently with your instructor. Aim to go out at a quiet time rather than brave the rush-hour traffic.

> *I drifted round on a fluffy pink-edged cloud of happiness for about an hour after passing my test before deciding it was time to take the plunge and go out by myself. I drove to a lovely riverside café not far from where I lived – you can't get there by public transport so I'd never been able to go independently before. I had a coffee and drove home again. It was such a wonderful, liberating experience.* Abigail, 27

> *My first drive was to an evening class I taught at a school a couple of miles away. It felt eerily quiet in the car and I kept wondering, 'Am I really allowed to do this?' I was holding my breath because I was so tense, and whenever I stopped at traffic lights I'd give this huge sigh of relief. But at the same time it was completely fantastic. I was used to cycling that route with my books and teaching materials in a ruck-sack and being able to just chuck everything into the car was bliss!* Naomi, 34

Fear of driving

There aren't any official figures for this but there's plenty of anecdotal evidence to suggest that some women, having passed their test, never or rarely drive afterwards. There can be a variety of reasons for this. A common one is that they pass their test at seventeen, then go off to college and can't afford to have a car of their own for several years. By the time they're able to buy one their skills have become rusty and they're not confident about driving alone. Other drivers never feel comfortable behind the wheel.

I was terrified during my lessons, especially at busy junctions or on dual carriageways. But I forced myself to go through with them because learning to drive at seventeen was expected in my family. I managed to scrape a pass but have never wanted to drive again, even though my parents offered to buy me a car. I'm a fairly confident person in other areas of my life but driving just freaks me out. Frances, 30

For many drivers the answer is having a few refresher lessons. But for others the problem runs deeper. It could be linked to family attitudes about driving, having been involved in a car accident or being pushed to take your test before you're ready. Dr Joshua Carritt-Baker is a clinical psychologist who, together with his driving instructor father, runs a service for anxious drivers combining counselling and driving sessions (see 'Reference Section' for details). 'There's this idea that we shouldn't feel anxious about driving,' he says. 'People often believe that everyone else is confident and give themselves a hard time about not being the same – but actually it's quite a common problem, it's just that it's very rarely discussed.'

The solution is to get more practice with an instructor or trusted companion and then build up to going on short, easy journeys alone. 'If you do something regularly your anxiety will reduce,' says Dr Carritt-Baker. 'Initially it can feel uncomfortable, but we work with clients offering them techniques such as breathing exercises or affirmations like "My driving is fine" or "My fear isn't going to hurt me" to help them stick at it.'

Accepting what sort of driver you're going to be is also helpful. Just because you're now qualified to go round the M25 in the dark doesn't mean you've got to. Maybe you'll just stick to local driving and take the train for longer journeys. But having gone through the expensive slog of getting your licence, never driving at all would be a pity. It's worth facing up to your fears and getting the help you need to build your confidence so you can enjoy the convenience and fun that driving brings.

Getting into the groove

Over the next few months, it's a good idea to go on a variety of drives to build up your experience and confidence. Trying different routes is important because if you just stick to commuting and socializing locally, you'll feel really daunted when you're confronted with the prospect of a four-hour motorway drive to get to a wedding or conference. It's during this time that you'll also learn what it is to navigate, park and fill up with petrol – all by yourself. Here are some tips for making it all run as smoothly as possible.

Navigation and journey planning

As a new driver it can feel very strange not to have someone there giving you directions any more. If you want to go to a particular place, you have to figure out the route yourself. Navigating can be a fraught business, even for the experienced driver. You'll discover for yourself how easy it can be to miss your particular turn-off and have to drive for miles before you find a place to turn round, about how hopeless people's directions can be, and the bewilderment of getting lost down a maze of narrow country roads where the idea of road signs appears to have been dispensed with altogether.

Preparation is very important for any journey, but particularly when you're a new driver.

- Plan your journey beforehand. As well as studying a map, you might also like to look at the route-finding services on the AA and RAC websites. They will suggest the best door-to-door route for you and also give you an approximate journey time – though as a new driver you should allow rather more than this.
- So that you won't have to constantly refer to your map, it can be useful to write sections of the route on Post-its, stick them on the dashboard of your car and then tear them off as you pass each point.
- If you need to refer to your map or directions then pull over, rather than trying to do it as you're driving along or at traffic lights.
- Don't allow people to give you directions that are of a non-specific nature such as 'Turn right at the roundabout as you're coming into town and then you'll pass a newsagent. . . .' If you get lost, pulling over and asking passers-by with only this to go on isn't going to be much use. What you want in addition are specific street names, pub names and major landmarks such as cinemas or police stations that you can look out for to make sure you're on the right track.
- If you're setting off on a long journey, make sure you leave plenty of time and that you've checked your water, oil, tyres and filled up with petrol beforehand. Your first lengthy trips can feel quite demanding, and you don't want any worries that might distract you from the road.
- Listen to the traffic reports beforehand and tune into them when you're on the road. If there are any accidents or hold-ups on your planned route you can consider changing it or at least allow more time for your journey.

☞ Take a break every two hours. Drink strong coffee and get fresh air into the car if you start to feel tired.

☞ It's a good idea to join one of the breakdown services so they can come to rescue you if your car gives out.

Parking

As a non-driver, parking isn't an issue. Buses drop you off at the stop, taxis will double-park and you can jump out. Easy. But once you're driving around on your own, all those moany remarks you've overheard people make in the past about how 'It's so difficult to park round there' or 'We had to go for miles to find a parking space' suddenly start to makes sense.

Many places are relatively trouble free. Supermarket car parks, for example, tend to have plenty of spaces, though you might have to park in the far reaches of them. They can be quite good destinations for your first few drives, simply because of their straighforwardness in this department.

City-centre car parks can get very full at peak times. It's important to be careful in multistorey ones as vehicles tend to be packed in closely and there are lots of concrete pillars you could potentially scrape against. When you're leaving it's easy to end up following the wrong set of arrows and find yourself climbing to higher and higher floors rather than out into the road. Don't panic though – just keep going and eventually you'll find somewhere there's enough space for you to turn around.

Street parking in city centres can be particularly challenging, especially as there's likely to be a lot of other traffic around. And some residential areas can be tricky too – such as terraces where all the cars are parked bumper to bumper, not only near the house you're visiting but in lots of adjoining streets, so you have to cruise fruitlessly around for ages trying to find a space.

Parking tends to feel more of a hurdle at the beginning of your driving career as you'll probably be a bit underconfident about testing out your parallel-parking skills in the real world and be hoping for a nice long several-car space that you can drive into rather than having to attempt to reverse into a small one, fail dismally while holding up a stream of traffic that's appeared from nowhere and then drive away again, trying to give off an unconcerned 'Well, I didn't really want to park there anyway, actually', vibe.

Having a friend in the car when you're trying to park might help you feel calmer. On the other hand it could make you more flustered and self-conscious – if that's the case with you then make them get out and go on ahead.

Have faith it won't always be like this. As you become more experienced you'll find your parking will improve and you'll be able to squeeze confidently into spaces that would once have daunted you.

However, you'll also realize that every so often life does throw up unusually tricky parking situations that leave you feeling every bit as much of a plank as you did when you first attempted it as a learner. Such as coming back to your car to discover that you've been boxed in and no amount of nifty manoeuvring will get you out again. There's no easy answer to this one, sadly, other than trying to hunt down the owners of the relevant cars and get one of them to move. And if that doesn't work, then you'll just have to go home on the bus and come back the following day by which time one of the inconsiderate twerps will hopefully have left. Or you could just find yourself defeated by a teeny-weeny, dolls-house version of a parking space.

> *I went to visit a client and was told parking was really bad round there but they'd booked me a space in their underground car park. I found the designated space, but it was tiny and there was hardly any room for manoeuvre so I was there for ages reversing back and forth, trying to get in. Eventually this security guard came down and said, 'We've been watching you for the past fifteen minutes on the CCTV and I wondered if you needed any help.' He had to guide me in, very embarrassing.*
> Siobhan, 29

And then, of course, there's the scenario where you've parked in a muddy field at a music festival or agricultural show and returned to find that moving off from the sodden ground is too much for your car. This is a time for even the most independent of girls to call upon male assistance. Even skinny-jeaned indie whippet-type blokes can prove remarkably useful when it comes to pushing a car out of mud, and if you're somewhere full of burly rockers or strapping young farmers then you're laughing.

If you park illegally you'll probably get a parking ticket and have to pay a fine, though it can get a lot worse than that in some locations where clamping and towing are the parking punishments of choice. So check the road signs very carefully before leaving your car, and bear in mind that in some places signs can be ambiguous and roads poorly marked. If you're in any doubt at all it's best to move on and find somewhere else to park.

If you do get fined just stump up and put it down to experience rather than turn into one of those people who gets all bitter and rants endlessly at the gross injustice. After all, the regulations are there for a purpose – for safety reasons, to ease congestion or to protect residents' parking rights. And it's worth remembering that parking in disabled spaces without a blue badge is particularly bad for your karma.

And when you've parked your car, don't forget you've got to find it again!

If you're the forgetful type, it's a good idea to make a note of where you've parked. It's awful if it slips your mind and you come back from a shopping trip or night out and have to wander round the nearby streets looking for your car, wondering anxiously what you'll do if you can't track it down. Maybe have posters of your beloved motor put up on trees and lampposts with a phone number and offer of a reward, like people do with lost pets? If you're at a big event like an outdoor gig then tying a brightly coloured ribbon or a balloon to the car aerial can help you track it down again.

Filling up

Hopefully you'll have had some experience of filling up with petrol with your driving instructor or when out practising, but doing it for the first time by yourself can still feel like a rite of passage.

Before going to the petrol station, check which side the petrol cap is on your car. When you pull in, this is the side you need to have close to the pump.

It's very important to know whether the car takes petrol or diesel. According to a study carried out by the AA Foundation, filling up with the wrong fuel is a mistake made by about 120,000 drivers each year, and you really don't want to be one of them. It can seriously damage your car's engine and cost from £80 to thousands of pounds to put right!

It's also a good idea to have a few goes at putting the petrol cap on and off before you set off. Some of them can be a bit fiddly and it's best to either get help or work out the knack for yourself at home rather than getting all flustered on the forecourt. If you really have problems getting the cap back on and there's no one around to help, it's possible to buy rubber replacement ones to tide you over at most petrol stations.

Don't smoke or use your mobile near the pumps as both are dangerous.

When you've filled up you'll need to go into the petrol station and pay, so make a note of which pump you used. Some petrol stations have credit card facilities right next to the pump, so they're worth looking out for.

It's a good idea to carry extra fuel in an approved container.

Checking and adjusting your tyre pressures

You should check your tyre pressures every week or so, and definitely do it before a long journey. It's something you need to do when the tyres are cold because after a long journey the readings will be different. Your car manual will tell you what they should be for the front and back wheels of your particular model, and it's possible to buy a little pen-shaped gadget from Halfords for under a fiver which lets you check your pressures at home without the hassle of going to a garage.

If they're not what they should be, then you'll need to inflate your tyres. There are machines for doing this on many petrol station forecourts, and as it can be quite a fiddly procedure it's a good idea to have someone there to guide you through it the first time.

Checking your tyre pressures is something best done when you're casually (or better still, scruffily) dressed as it does involve a lot of grovelling around on the petrol station forecourt getting stained and grimy. It's not something to attempt when you've gone for that Liz Hurley immaculate white jeans and heels look.

Automatic car wash

These fall into two main types. The first is the drive-through type which you drive into, switch the engine off and are shunted slowly through while your car is scrubbed and hosed from all directions. Remembering to close the windows beforehand is vital here. The other type has various brushes and hoses which you wield yourself, having pressed the relevant buttons for a blast of soap and water, waxing agent or water to rinse the car down.

Many car washes don't accept coins and you have to get tokens from the garage shop beforehand, so check the situation out before you get started. Like many car-care related tasks, using an automatic car wash is actually quite simple, but it's easy to get flustered when you haven't done it before. So aim to choose a quiet time of day for your first attempt.

Night driving

If you haven't done much night driving with your instructor, it can come as a bit of a shock to the system. And it's worth bearing in mind that there are different sorts of night driving. Cruising along at 30 m.p.h. in a built-up area with lots of street lamps is a different matter from driving along a pitch-black country lane, and different again from a busy dual carriageway, being dazzled by oncoming headlights and dealing with pressure from drivers behind to go faster.

There's no doubt that driving at night is more dangerous. A DfT (STATS 19) study in 2004 revealed that although only about 15 per cent of vehicle miles are clocked up between 7 p.m. and 7 a.m., they account for almost a third of road injuries and deaths. This is because of reduced visibility and because there are more drivers on the road who are under the influence of drink or drugs.

- If you don't take a Pass Plus course, at least make sure you do a few sessions of night driving with your instructor and make sure you experience the different varieties.
- Make sure your lights and windows are clean – this makes a tremendous difference!
- Even if you feel hassled to go faster by other drivers, only go at a speed where you can stop safely within the distance you can see in your headlights.
- If you're in danger of being dazzled by the headlights of oncoming cars, keep your eye on the left kerb, so you don't drive towards them.
- If you don't like night driving, keep it to a minimum at first and build up your experience gradually.

Bright sunlight

Most people are aware that night driving can be difficult, but being dazzled by sunlight can come as a surprise. On sunny days it's important to be aware of where the sun is and when you might turn into it. Keep the sun visor down on bright days and if you do find yourself dazzled, slow down and wriggle around to see if a change of position can keep it out of your eyes. It's also essential to keep all your windows clean inside and out to cut down on dazzle. Always keep a spare pair of good quality polarized sunglasses in your car, so you don't ever find yourself on the road without them.

Dealing with emergency vehicles

Hearing a siren or seeing a flashing blue light in your rear-view mirror can throw many drivers into panic mode. However, it's not as scary as it seems. Remember the driver of the emergency vehicle is an expert and will be used to negotiating situations like this, so just stay calm, slow down and pull in at the side of the road as soon as you safely can. If you're in the outside lane of a dual carriageway, other drivers tend to be good about creating space for you to pull into the inside lane. However, do try to think things through and don't stop on a narrow section of road that won't allow the ambulance or police car to go past you. If you find yourself in this situation, drive on a bit further until the road widens.

Being careful out there

Hopefully your driving career will be trouble-free. But it's important to assume responsibility for yourself and take all the steps you can to make sure you and your passengers stay safe. Here are some important points to bear in mind.

Don't get lazy

Once they've passed their test, many people start to let careless driving habits such as poor observations or lack of respect for the speed limit creep in. Make sure this doesn't happen to you. 'When my students pass their test I always tell them, "It takes a lot of commitment to stay as good as you are now,"' says driving instructor Liz Mitchell. Continuing to drive as you've been taught is one of the most important steps to staying safe on the road.

Mobile phones

It's good to have your mobile with you and charged up for safety reasons, but it's best to keep it switched off. A study called Driving at Work carried out by the Health and Safety Executive in 2003 revealed that drivers are four times more likely to be involved in an accident when using a mobile phone.

The use of hand-held mobile phones while driving was banned in December 2003 and if you're caught using one you'll get points on your licence. However, hands-free models can also have a negative effect on your driving because the conversation distracts you from what's happening on the road. So no matter how addicted to your mobile you are, turn it off when driving. There will never be a call or text message that's worth risking someone's life for.

Alcohol

When you're driving, it's best to avoid alcohol completely. The legal limit is a blood alcohol level of 80 mg/100 ml but even an amount that's well under that limit can affect your co-ordination and make accidents more likely. And staying 'under the limit' is a really tricky business. Different types of beers, wines and alcopops have varying strengths, the effect varies depending on your weight, metabolism and whether you've eaten recently, and if you're at a party you'll probably be offered a drink that has two or three times more alcohol than you'd get in a pub measure.

Drink-driving can have tragic consequences. The *Road Casualties Great Britain: 2004 Annual Report* published by the DfT revealed that 17 per cent of all fatal accidents involved drivers over the legal alcohol limit. And it's a problem that's getting worse – the numbers of people killed or injured by drink-drivers have both increased by more than a third over the past decade.

Even if you're not involved in an accident, the penalty for driving over the limit is automatic disqualification for at least a year, though this can be longer at the court's discretion. They are also allowed to impose a fine of up to £5000 and a prison sentence of up to six months.

So it's best to start your driving career as you mean to go on and make a commitment to never, ever drink and drive. Although it might seem a bit harsh initially, you'll find that taking a zero-tolerance attitude actually makes life easier. There's no dithering about 'Ooh, will I be all right with just a small one?' or trying to stop people from topping up your glass. You know you're either sticking to soft drinks or making other arrangements to get home. As you get used to it, you'll find your own way of making this approach work without leaving you feeling too deprived. Here are some tips to get you started:

- Do an analysis of your social life and work out the times when having a drink makes a real difference to your enjoyment and those when it wouldn't matter. For example, you might be happy to stick to soft drinks on a night out with your girlfriends, but really miss not being able to get a bit plastered at a party or gig. That way you can drive some of the time and save your money for splashing out on taxis at others. Track down some bars that serve smoothies, a variety of coffees or groovy non-alcoholic cocktails and arrange to meet your mates there on the nights you're avoiding booze.
- If you're on a diet remind yourself that alcohol tends to be high in calories and cutting back on it means more opportunity to indulge in chips or chocolate.
- If you're the chauffeur for the evening and find yourself dourly surveying your mineral water or orange juice, feeling all cheated and hard-done-by, promise yourself a winding-down glass of wine in front of some late-night junk TV when you get home.
- Arranging a lift home from a non-drinking mate is great, but always be aware that the situation might change. They might want to leave later or earlier than you, take a detour via some dubious-sounding party or their car might break down. They might decide to drink after all, and you could realise that you wouldn't feel safe being their passenger. Always have backup in the form of a number of a reliable cab firm and your fare home on you.
- Better still, always have the number of several cab firms in your mobile – that way you've got a better chance of finding one that can pick you up fairly promptly.

If you stay somewhere overnight and plan to drive home in the morning, you need to be aware that if you've drunk a lot you may well still be over the limit the following day. On average, it takes one hour per unit plus one hour for alcohol to leave your system. So given that one unit of alcohol is a small pub measure of wine, if you've had two glasses, it'll take three hours to leave your system, four glasses will take five hours and a bottle of wine (six small glasses) will take seven hours. If you're concerned that you might still be over the limit, take public transport home or into work, or have breakfast and go out for a walk until the alcohol has left your system.

Drugs

Hopefully you're not the sort of girl who would even consider taking hard drugs in the first place, let alone driving afterwards. But it's important not to be even tempted to share a joint that's going around at a party, it'll slow your reactions and will be highly dangerous once you're behind the wheel. Increasingly, the police are taking blood and urine tests from drivers they suspect of being under the influence of drugs, so don't think the fact you'd pass a breathalyser test will protect you from prosecution.

Your passengers

Choose your passengers carefully. Studies have shown that young drivers carrying young passengers are at far greater risk on the road and this risk increases with every additional passenger. For example, a survey by Drs Regan and Mitsopoulos, carried out at the Monash University Accident Research

Centre in Australia in 2003, revealed that the risk of a young driver having a crash increased five times if they had young passengers, particularly male ones. This is because the other passengers, especially if they're drunk, can egg the driver on to take risks or go faster and even go in for dimwitted horseplay such as putting their hands over the driver's eyes or mucking around with the handbrake. If you suspect anyone you know might be inconsiderate enough to behave like this, make them take the bus. You might even want to smirk in a superior fashion as you drive by. And if you find yourself giving a lift to friends of friends who play up, then pull over and make it clear you're not going any further until they stop being such idiots.

Personal safety for girls on the go

Most women tend to feel much safer in their cars than they do using public transport. But don't let that make you complacent. Although road rage, carjacking and being attacked when in or approaching your car are thankfully rare, it's wise to take simple precautions to keep yourself safe. The Suzy Lamplugh Trust (see 'Reference Section' for details) has excellent advice on driving safety, but here are some basic guidelines:

- Always make sure your car is in good working order and there's no risk of running out of fuel.
- Always keep your car doors locked when you're driving along.

- If someone in another car tries to attract your attention, ignore them and avoid making eye contact.
- If you think you're being followed drive to a police station or somewhere busy such as a pub or service station and phone for help from there.
- Don't pick up hitchhikers.
- Avoid 'road rage' situations – don't shout at or deliberately obstruct other drivers, and do your best to ignore it if they shout at or obstruct you.
- If you see an accident or incident, think before you automatically stop to help. Ask yourself if it might not be better to ring the police.
- If a car pulls in front of you and forces you to stop, keep your engine running. Ensure your doors and windows are locked. If the driver leaves their car to approach you, try to reverse as far as possible and drive away. Put your hazard lights on and sound your horn as well.
- If you break down, phone for help. You should then stay in your car, unless you're on the hard shoulder of the motorway in which case you should wait on the verge. However, if another driver pulls up nearby, get into your car and lock the doors and windows. If they offer help, explain it's already on its way.
- Some police authorities run short courses on coping with road rage and safe driving for women, which can be well worth attending.

Parking safety

- Think ahead when you're parking. If you're parking in daylight but will return after dark, ask yourself what the area might be like then. If you think you might feel isolated or threatened, find somewhere else to park.

- Reverse into parking bays, as it'll be easier to get away briskly.
- If you're using a multistorey car park and there's an attendant, try to park near his booth.
- If possible use a 'secured car park'. These are approved by the Association of Police Officers. Look at www.secured carparks.com to find one near you.
- Keep valuables out of sight and, in particular, don't let your car reveal it belongs to a woman – stow heels, handbags, etc. out of sight.
- Ask a friend or colleague to walk you to your car if you feel apprehensive.
- When you return to your car, have your keys ready, check the back seat before you get in and then lock the doors immediately.

Accidents

Hopefully your driving career will be accident free. But if you're involved in an accident where people or animals are injured or property is damaged then everyone involved should exchange their name, address and insurance details. If there are any independent witnesses, get their details too. The law does require you to give your address but if the other person is a bit scary and road-ragy, and you're afraid to let them know where you live, then one option would be to just supply your phone number, work address and insurance details initially, then get in touch with the police and give your full address to them, letting them know why you didn't want to reveal it at the scene.

If you're not able to do so at the time – you've scraped someone's car and the owner isn't around, for example – it's a legal requirement to make a note of the time, place and number plate of the car and report it to the police as soon as possible – leaving a note under the windscreen wiper with your contact details isn't enough. It's also advisable to draw a sketch plan of the scene and take photos from different angles if you've got a camera or cameraphone with you. You should also report the accident to your insurer even if you're not intending to make a claim. This is a requirement of virtually every motor insurance policy, as is never admitting liability at the scene (it'll be covered in the boring small print in the insurance policy document that you never got round to reading).

If you're the sort of girl who apologizes when someone else stands on your foot, resisting the urge to take the blame could feel difficult. This is actually a widespread problem for women. The DfT Cohort Study of Learner and Novice Drivers 2003 noted that women blame themselves for accidents that aren't their fault far more than men. But stay neutral at this point and let it be sorted out through the official channels.

If you only have third party insurance and the collision wasn't your fault, you can claim from whoever was legally liable for the damage. Your insurance company can give you advice on how to go about this. However, you'll have to be able to prove their negligence beyond reasonable doubt, so the more backup information you can acquire at the time, the better.

Be wary of anyone who says, 'Let's just sort this out between ourselves and leave the insurance companies out of it.' It's important to report any incident to your company as the other person could come back to you later and ask for more money for the damage than they originally mentioned. Going through your insurance company will protect your interests if things get awkward further down the line.

If you're involved in a collision with an uninsured motorist you should report the incident both to your own insurance company and to the police, and they'll advise you on what to do.

If your car is stolen, then inform the police and your insurance company.

Getting your L-plates back again

You've worked so hard to get rid of your L-plates – it would be unthinkably horrible to get them back. But if you don't drive responsibly, it could happen. Imagine how grim it would be to have to take your test again and so be cautious out there.

The New Drivers Act – tremble before it!

The New Drivers Act 1995 means that if you accumulate six or more penalty points during your first two years of driving your licence will be revoked. You will then need to retake your theory and practical tests. Bearing in mind that you get a minimum of three penalty points for speeding, it only takes two such offences and you can say goodbye to your precious licence. Something to bear in mind when you're in a hurry and are tempted to push the speed limit or commit another driving offence.

I got some points on my licence for speeding, and then some more for parking too near to a zebra crossing, and lost my licence. I'm having to retake my test and the cost of the test combined with the extra lessons means I can't go on holiday this year. I have never felt more stupid in my life. Clare, 19

The extended driving test – this is even worse!

If you're convicted of dangerous driving, you will lose your licence and after a period of disqualification may have to take an extended driving test in order to drive again. It's longer than the regular test (seventy minutes rather than forty) and more demanding. Also, just think what it would be like to take a driving test not as an ordinary learner but as someone whom the examiner would know had misbehaved badly in the past.

Losing your licence

Drivers who accumulate twelve or more penalty points on their licence over a three-year period will be disqualified from driving for a minimum of six months. This doesn't necessarily involve retaking your test, but it would mean you'd be back waiting at the bus stop. And once you were able to drive again you'd discover that your car insurance premiums had rocketed.

L

Buying your first car

If you're able to buy a car after passing your test, you're about to embark on a very special relationship. Like their first love, everyone remembers their first car. But while memories of the object of one's earliest passion can bring up a variety of emotions such as pain, regret or (most frequently) embarrassment, even the most hardened cynics have only to think of their first car and they're enveloped in a haze of shiny-eyed doting nostalgia. It might have been a rusty old Ford Escort, but it was *their* rusty old Ford Escort and by experiencing their first taste of the fun and freedom of driving in its company it will have won a place in their heart for ever.

So don't rush into this relationship. Take your time and aim to track down a car that you'll feel safe in and that won't break your heart through high repair bills. Unfortunately, this is easier said than done as car buying is by no means an exact science. Cars that are similar in terms of price and reputation can end up behaving very differently – one might be reliable and loyal while another could turn out to be temperamental and expensive to maintain. Particularly at the second-hand end of the market, there's a real luck-of-the-draw element to it. Your best bet for success is to do your research thoroughly. Ask everyone you know who's even slightly switched-on about cars what they'd get if they had your requirements and budget.

There are three main options:

- Buying from a private sale – such as through *Auto Trader* or the local newspaper. It's possible to get some real bargains this way, but it's important to have the car checked out by someone who really knows about motors as legally there's very little comeback if it turns out to be a crock.

- Buying from a dealership – they tend to offer a guarantee for at least a few months, so you'll have the chance to see if any problems develop and get them fixed. Second-hand car dealers have a dodgy reputation, but there are some good ones out there – ask around among friends to see if there are any local dealers they'd recommend. Your driving instructor might also be able to advise you.

- Buying a new car – the new car market is very competitive, and there are plenty of special deals and discounts around. When you're buying a new car it's important to bear in mind depreciation (the loss in the car's value once you've bought it). Cars depreciate at different rates and the difference between the best and the worst depreciators can run into thousands. *WhatCar* magazine is an excellent source of advice on buying new cars, and also has a depreciation index on its website at www.whatcar.com

Getting even better

Probably the thought of more lessons is the last thing on your mind at the moment. But in the future you might want to look at ways you can improve your driving.

- Skid control lessons can be really useful, especially if you live in a part of the country which tends to get a lot of snow and ice.
- You might want to do an advanced driving course.

RoSPA and the Institute of Advanced Motorists (IAM) both run these and they can help you become a more skilful and confident driver. This is great for everyone but particularly important if you drive a lot for work. They can also bring your insurance down significantly, especially if you're under twenty-five.

● Vehicle maintenance courses can be a worthwhile investment. Being able to do your own basic checks and repairs will save you money and knowing what goes on under the bonnet can help you avoid being ripped off by unscrupulous garages. And if you're a single girl, it also doubles as a classic strategy for meeting men.

If you'd just like to have some fun, it's possible to get gift vouchers for sessions driving a racing car, a Ferrari – or even a tank! Drop hints to your family and friends when your birthday or Christmas comes round.

The open road

Having a driving licence is every bit as wonderful as it's cracked up to be – and more. The route to getting it could have been relatively easy or so arduous that there were times when you wondered if you'd ever make it. But you did. You've cleared a hurdle that some people find one of the most daunting and acquired a skill that will benefit you for the rest of your life.

Whether you use your licence to travel the length of the country and beyond or are happy to just potter about on local trips, it will give you a level of freedom, independence and convenience that's impossible to grasp as a non-driver. Even if you can't afford to own a car right away, you'll be able to drive company vehicles, drive friends' or family's cars, hire one on holiday or get behind the wheel in an emergency.

Passing your test gives you a sense of life opening up. You're not tied to train or bus timetables any longer and you've got more options. You can live in the depths of the countryside, get a job that involves driving, travel up mountains or nip off to visit friends at a moment's notice. There's a fun and fabulous driving future lying ahead of you. Enjoy it!

Chapter 10

Car Insurance Without Tears

Well, let's not get too optimistic. Finding out about and getting the best deal on car insurance is a hateful, tedious, time-consuming, life-sapping activity that will make your head hurt. But despite this, it's not a waste of time. Getting the right cover means you can feel confident that if you do have the bad luck to be involved in an accident, the financial impact and general inconvenience will be kept to a minimum. And shopping around for the best deal can save you hundreds of pounds.

However, if you've never done it before then plunging headfirst into calling up companies for quotes can leave you with the disturbing feeling of having been airlifted down to Planet Car Insurance. A place where everyone speaks a different language in which they only say really boring things. The person at the other end of the phone will start talking about 'voluntary excess' and 'third party', blithely assuming that you've got a clue what they're talking about.

As a learner driver, your first venture into this fascinating world is likely to involve getting yourself covered for supervised practice driving. This usually involves becoming a 'named driver' for someone else's car, or getting a car of your own to practise in. If you're taking the 'named driver' option then many of the variables, such as the make of car or where it's kept, are going to be out of your control, so your grounding in car insurance basics doesn't need to be anything like as thorough as someone who's planning on buying a car.

But whether you're a learner or a new driver, have a car of your own or are on someone else's policy, it's still worthwhile to get up to speed on the terms insurers use and the sometimes sensible, sometimes twisted reasoning behind the questions they ask. It also has psychological benefits in that you get to feel mature and shrewd and worldly rather than bewildered and inadequate. So make yourself a cup of tea and plough through the following. Put Destiny's Child's 'Independent Woman' on in the background if you think that might help.

You what? How to understand what people are saying when they talk to you about car insurance

Insurance premium – This is the cost of insuring your own car. It can vary hugely depending on factors such as your age, driving experience, where you live and the type of car. It's not unusual for new drivers to discover they'll be paying more for their first year's car insurance than they did for their actual car. It's very unpleasant when this happens, one of those real 'loss of innocence' moments.

Cover note – This acts as a temporary policy and certificate until your new insurance policy has been fully set up.

Certificate of insurance – This is your formal evidence of insurance and you should get it shortly after taking your policy out. You'll need this to buy your road tax disc.

Policy document – This is the document packed with confusing small print that sets out the full terms and conditions of your policy. Mistakes and misunderstandings can turn out to be very expensive further down the line. So grit your teeth and read the wretched thing. If there's anything in it you don't fully understand, call the company up straight away and get them to explain it to you.

The policyholder – The main driver of the car.

Named driver – This is an extra driver who uses the car less than the main driver. Usually the named driver can use it for leisure but not regular commuting. If you're practising on a boyfriend's or family member's car, or if you'll want to use it after you've passed, you'll need to be put on as a named driver.

'Fronting' – This is a slang term for a bad thing you mustn't do, which is get a car of your own and have a more experienced driver (say, your mum) on as the main driver and yourself as a named driver, when actually you're the one who uses it most. This arrangement can be cheaper in terms of insurance costs but it's actually fraud. If you ever need to make a claim, insurance companies will investigate the situation and if they realize that 'fronting' has been going on then your policy can be declared invalid. You'll then be responsible for all the costs of the accident yourself and could also find it difficult to get insurance in the future.

Pay as you drive car insurance – This is a new approach to car insurance pioneered by Norwich Union. It uses the latest Global Positioning Satellite (GPS) technology to calculate your monthly insurance premiums based on how often, when and where you drive; which means that if you do a lower mileage, or don't do any night driving, you're seen as a lower risk and hence are offered cheaper premiums. A small smart box with its own GPS tracking system is fitted into your car, your journeys are monitored by a central computer and your monthly premiums calculated on that basis. If you're not likely to clock up serious mileage, it's certainly worth looking into.

Types of cover

Third party – This is the minimum insurance you need to drive legally in the UK. It covers your legal liability to pay damages to other people for injury to themselves, their passengers and their property. It doesn't pay out for damage to your car or your medical expenses if you're injured. However, if the accident is proven to be the other party's fault their insurance should pay.

Third party fire and theft – This gives the above cover and will also pay out if your car is stolen or catches fire.

Fully comprehensive – This covers your liability to a third party, fire and theft. It also covers damage to you and your own car. It should pay for any repairs or a replacement car if yours is written off.

Some insurance companies will only authorize repairs by a garage named by them (approved repairers). This can be convenient as it means you don't have to trail around for quotes. However, if you feel a strong allegiance to your own garage, then you might want to choose a policy which allows you to decide where repairs are carried out.

Bear in mind that if your car is written off or stolen, you won't necessarily get what you paid for it. It's more usual to be offered the current market value for a car of that age and type.

Additional cover

Here are some other benefits which could be included in your policy, or which you might want to arrange as 'add-on' cover.

Motor legal expenses – This will cover your legal expenses if, for example, you're involved in an accident that isn't your fault and you need to claim your uninsured losses, such as your excess or the cost of a replacement car, from the other party.

Temporary replacement car – Sometimes referred to as a 'courtesy car'. If having your car off the road after an accident would cause you serious problems, then you might want to take out cover that would provide you with a car while your own is being repaired or replaced.

Personal belongings – If you regularly travel with a suitcase full of designer clothes or carry expensive sports equipment or your laptop in your car you might want to consider being insured against their theft. However, these items could already be covered on your home insurance policy, so check that first. There's no point in insuring things twice!

Driving other cars insurance – This covers the policy-holder when driving other people's cars with their permission, but cover is generally limited to third party only, and only in emergency situations.

Breakdown cover – Some insurance companies will encourage you to take out breakdown cover with them as well. However, this might not be the best deal for you – shop around and get some quotes from breakdown companies such as the AA or RAC as well.

Excess

Compulsory excess – This is the amount set by the insurer that you will pay on any claim before their contribution kicks in. So let's say you drive into someone else's car causing £250 damage, and your compulsory excess is £100 – you pay £100 and your insurers pay out £150. However, you might choose not to claim on your insurance policy and pay the whole of the £250 yourself. The motivation here would be to protect your no-claims bonus (of which more later).

Young driver excess – Insurers almost always make young drivers pay an extra excess on top of the standard compulsory excess – typically it's an extra £250 until twenty-one, then reducing to £150 until twenty-five.

Voluntary excess – Is an amount that you might offer to pay, in addition to the compulsory excess. Offering to chip in more in this way (a voluntary excess of £150, £200, £250 or whatever) can lower the cost of your premium.

No-claims discount (sometimes called no-claims bonus) – Policyholders with a claim-free record can claim a discount on their insurance. Discounts vary between insurers but can reach a maximum of about 60 per cent after five or six years. So a basic insurance premium of, say, £700 can be reduced to £280. It's savings like these that make people so keen on their no-claims discount and so willing to jump through hoops to protect it.

If you're insuring your own car, then you can start building up your no-claims discount even as a learner driver. As a general rule you can't get it as a named driver on someone else's car, though some companies, such as Directline, are beginning to offer this. It's also sometimes possible to get one based on company car experience.

L

Factors which influence the cost of car insurance

The type of cover

As you might expect, fully comprehensive is the most expensive. If you're a young or inexperienced driver, then the cost can be very high. And if your car is an old banger, then getting insurance cover to repair it or replace it if it's stolen might actually end up costing more than the car is worth, which may well mean that third party would be a better bet.

Many new drivers start off with third party and then work up to fully comprehensive when they've had a few years' experience and their insurance becomes cheaper. However, if you do go for third party only, you might want to consider having add-on cover for motor legal expenses to supplement it. It's also worth getting quotes for additional benefits you'd like, such as a replacement car, and weighing up whether they're important enough to you to fork out for.

Your cover as a learner or new driver – If you're insuring your own car, the type of cover you go for is up to you. If you're going on your mum's or boyfriend's insurance as a named driver you'll generally be offered the same sort of cover (third party fire and theft, fully comprehensive, etc.) that they have. If you want any changes or supplements, then discuss this with the insurance company to see if that's possible.

The car

The insurance group (ABI group) – Whenever a new car is developed, the manufacturers deliver sample models for testing at the insurance industries test centre. Safety features such as air bags and seat designs are evaluated, they look at how the car performs in crash tests, the engine power, the cost of repairs and parts and security features such as alarms and immobilizers. Then a panel of experts agrees a group rating.

The insurance groups currently go from 1–20 – the lowest being the cheaper cars to insure. Although a lot of factors are taken into consideration, basically the high-performance cars are in the higher groups. Here are some examples:

- Citroën 2CV – group 1
- Ford Focus – about 4–8
- A 'hot hatchback' (a small hatchback car with a powerful engine) such as a VW Golf GTI – about 14–15
- Porsche 911 Carrera – 20

You can find the insurance-group rating of a car on the manufacturer's website or at www.parkers.co.uk or www.glass.co.uk.

The age of the car – Learner drivers often think that it's a good idea to get an old banger to practise on as it'll be cheaper to insure, but that's not always the case. Some older cars can be difficult to get replacement parts for, which makes them more expensive to repair. And as some of them don't respond as briskly as younger cars they can be more accident prone. Newer cars are also much safer in terms of protecting passengers. But on the other hand, there are older cars where cover is very reasonable. The only way to find out which category a car falls into is to get a quote specifically for it.

Security features – The more you can protect your car against theft, the lower your premium is likely to be. Keeping it in a garage or on a driveway overnight is seen as a definite plus. Car alarms and steering locks are also given a big thumbs-up by insurance companies.

Modifications – A car that's had modifications such as alloy wheels, tinted windows or spoilers fitted is likely to be more expensive to insure. This is because these 'pimping your ride' type of alterations are associated with boy racers. They also make the car more attractive to the sort of thieves who'll want to drive it round like nutcases, then set fire to it in a car park.

Your cover as a learner or new driver – If you're going on your parents' or boyfriend's car as a 'named driver', then obviously you won't have much control over what sort of a car it is. But if you've got a choice between being put on your mum's Nissan Micra or your dad's BMW, then the above information should help you understand why your mum's car would probably be the more economical choice. The prospect of a learner or new driver at the wheel of a high-performance motor is going to give most insurance companies an attack of the vapours and any quote is likely to be sky-high. But having said that, it would always be worth getting a quote for both vehicles. The fact that there are zillions of other factors the insurance company is going to take into consideration means you don't always get the answer you expect!

If you're thinking of buying a car to practise on or to drive after you've passed your test, then always check out what the insurance might be before going ahead with the purchase – you don't want to get any nasty surprises.

My neighbour was selling his VW Golf. I'd heard that VWs were nice, sensible sorts of cars, so I enquired about buying it to practise in. Luckily, he explained that it was a GTI, which meant it would go like the clappers and cost a fortune to insure. I'm quite an impulsive person so if I'd been buying it in a private sale I'd probably have just handed over the cash and then got a horrible shock when I called the insurance company. Naomi, 34

You

Your age – One of the few compensations for getting older is that your car insurance gets cheaper. Statistically, younger people have more accidents, so between seventeen and twenty you're seen as being particularly high-risk. At twenty-one premiums take a significant drop, and then again at twenty-five.

Your gender – Despite tiresome jokes about 'women drivers', our superior safety record is better reflected by cheaper car insurance. Though, as it happens, women do have roughly as many accidents as men. The difference is that women's accidents tend to be of the 'reversing into bollards' variety, whereas men are more likely to have crashes related to speed in which cars need extensive repairs or are even written off. Insurance quotes for women tend to be much lower than for men, especially young men, who have the worst safety record of all. For example, all other things being equal (location, mileage, history of car, etc.), a sample fully comprehensive quote for a 17-year-old girl driving a Peugeot 206 was £700, and £1200 for a 17-year-old boy.

Where you live – If you live in an area with a high crime rate your premium is going to be higher than if you're in a more law-abiding one because you're at greater risk of having your car stolen. Areas where there's a greater density of traffic also attract higher premiums as the idea is the more other cars there are knocking around, the higher the probability of you bumping into one or vice versa.

A common quandary for students is where to register their car if they spend part of the year at university and the holidays at home.

The quote for insuring my car at my parents' address in Bath was £800, but from my student house in Manchester, it's £1200. Jude, 21

It's not a good idea to choose the cheaper address and give that one, because if you need to make a claim the insurance company will almost certainly manage to work out your ruse and use it as an excuse to render your policy invalid and wriggle out of paying anything at all. When you call up for a quote explain the situation and ask for the fact that you divide your time between the two locations to be taken into consideration.

The mileage you do and what you use your car for ('type of use') – As a learner or new driver it can be difficult to work out what your expected mileage will be. As a learner you'll only be able to drive on journeys you can persuade someone to accompany you on. But once you've passed your test, it's up to you. You could find that the heady freedom of having your own car will have you travelling huge distances to see bands or long-lost friends every weekend. Or maybe you'll discover that long motorway drives aren't really your thing and just stick with commuting and modest local trips.

However, when you're first getting a quote you'll need to have a stab at estimating your mileage. Find out the distances you're likely to travel to work or to visit friends and add them up to a yearly total. Give the insurers that figure initially, otherwise the sales person will plug in an average of about 12,000 and if you do significantly less than that you could be paying more than you need. However, if you realize you're going to exceed the mileage you originally stated, let the insurers know as soon as possible

The insurers will also want to know what you'll be using the car for. 'Social domestic and pleasure', 'commuting' and 'business' are three possible options. It's important to be accurate about the 'type of use'. For example, if you say you use your car just for commuting, but then have an accident on the way to a business meeting in another location, then the company could refuse to pay out.

Your occupation – Insurance companies often take occupation into consideration when calculating premiums. If you're a journalist, barmaid or work in the entertainment industry, then you're seen as being more likely to drink and drive and to do a lot of night driving and hence be more at risk. If on the other hand you work in a bank, as a librarian or a teacher, then you're viewed as a safer prospect.

Your driving history – Premiums can be higher if you've had accidents in the past or have points on your licence. As a learner you may feel you haven't had much opportunity to blot your copybook yet – but some people manage it! If you've been convicted of a serious driving offence, such as drink-driving, then you are in serious trouble – your insurance is going to cost a fortune. Insurers might also only offer you limited cover; they'll insure you for third party but refuse to take you on for fully comprehensive.

Other drivers on the policy – If you go on parents'

insurance and they've got a good driving record it's likely that your presence on their insurance as a named driver will bump it up. How much will depend on factors such as your age. If, however, you go on your boyfriend's insurance you could both get a pleasant surprise. Even though you're a learner, you might actually bring it down! This is because couples are seen as more stable in the insurance industry. I suspect the general idea is that single men drive more recklessly because of all that excess testosterone, whereas a bloke with the good fortune to have found himself a girlfriend is likely to conduct himself in a more mellow fashion.

I'd already gone on my mum's insurance as a named driver and it had cost a fair bit. I was doubtful about going on my boyfriend's too as I didn't want to shell out any more cash. However, he'd offered to take me for practice drives so we looked into it – and discovered that getting me on his policy would actually reduce it by £30! Abigail, 27

If you're insuring your own car then having older, more experienced drivers such as your mum or partner on the policy can bring it down – even if the named driver only drives it infrequently it's seen as evening out the risk. Definitely look into this when you're getting quotes.

Taking the Pass Plus course – Many insurers offer insurance discounts of up to 30 per cent for new drivers who have taken this extra set of training sessions. It can also give you cheaper insurance as a named driver.

L

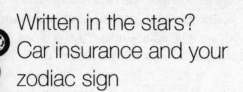

Written in the stars?
Car insurance and your
zodiac sign

The Australian insurance company Suncorp Metway carried out a study on 160,000 car accident claims between 2000 and 2004 and discovered that Geminis are the most likely to have an accident. 'Geminis, typically described as restless, easily bored and frustrated by things moving slowly, had more car accidents than any other sign,' said Warren Duke, Suncorp's National Manager, General Insurance. Sensible Capricorns came bottom in the accident stakes. The full list, starting with the most accident-prone star sign was as follows: Gemini, Taurus, Pisces, Virgo, Cancer, Aquarius, Aries, Leo, Libra, Sagittarius, Scorpio, Capricorn. Fortunately for Geminis, insurance companies aren't planning on taking zodiac signs into consideration when calculating premiums any time soon.

Top tips for researching car insurance as a learner or new driver

- Expect it to be a drag. When it comes to getting the right deal there are so many variables that even experienced drivers find it a nightmare. You're going to have to shop around for the best quote and giving your details to different companies can get tedious – but the money you're likely to save will make it time well spent.

- Some people are the kind who know loads about stuff like car insurance and it's generally easy to work out who they are. It's like it's in their aura or something. So if you can sense that your Uncle Bob or Karen from the IT department might be able to point you in the direction of some good deals, then don't hesitate to pick their brains.

- Being organized will really help. Get the information you'll need together before phoning: the details of the car you want insured (or the several cars you might want to check out before buying), your expected mileage and the level of cover you're after. And when comparing insurance quotes, make sure you're comparing like with like. Insurer A might make you an offer that's cheaper than insurer B but which doesn't include something that's important to you, such as insurance for your personal belongings.

- Don't assume you'll get a better quote from a company that specializes in women drivers – mostly it's just marketing hype. All insurers factor the statistics about women being safer drivers into their calculations.

- If you'd like to be taught by your instructor in or take your test in your or your parents' car, let the insurance company know at this stage and see what they have to say about it.

- If you're first getting quotes as a learner, check how your premium will change once you've passed your test.

- Get on the internet. It's the easiest way to do your initial research. www.confused.com and www.insuresuper market.com are both highly recommended sites that can help you find the right provider for you. Martin Lewis, a journalist and money-saving expert, runs a fantastic site www.moneysavingexpert.com that can give excellent advice on haggling for the best quote.

- When you're trying to bring your quote down, try out different scenarios such as 'What if I did a Pass Plus course?', 'What if I took a higher voluntary excess?', 'What if I fitted a car alarm?', 'What if I had my dad on as a named driver?', and see what effect it has on your premium.

- Be wary if the insurance company suggests paying your premium in monthly instalments. It might sound like a good idea but it generally isn't. Essentially what they're doing is loaning you the full amount upfront and then charging you a high rate (often up to 20 per cent) of interest on it. If you do need to take out a loan for your premium, you'll be able to find a much better deal by shopping around for one.

- Don't be in too much of a rush to sign up there and then. Most companies will hold your details while you take time to go through the different quotes you've had and then get back to them.

L

If anything changes, anything at all, tell your insurance company

After going through all the palaver of getting the right insurance policy you don't want to risk rendering it invalid by not keeping them up to date on any changes. This applies whether you're the main policyholder or a named driver. Here are some examples of the sort of things they'll want to hear about:

- If you have any accidents (even ones you're not going to make a claim for)
- If you change jobs or get a job after being a student
- If you move house
- When you pass your test
- If you start doing a higher mileage than you originally stated
- If you change the use of your vehicle – for example, from social domestic and pleasure to business use
- If you can't keep your car in a garage any more
- If you change your car engine, colour, seats or carry out any 'pimping your ride' modifications
- If you develop a health problem which might affect your driving
- If you get any criminal convictions or commit any driving offences
- If you're taking your car abroad
- If you split up with your boyfriend (though this is only relevant if he happens to be a named driver on your policy)

If the change is significant enough for the policy to need to be redrafted, then you might have to pay an administration fee of about £20. It's annoying, but necessary to keep your car insurance valid. Make sure they confirm their acknowledgement and acceptance of any changes in writing.

If you change cars

If your car conks out or you decide to sell it, then cancelling your policy can involve an administration charge of about £50. However, if you're planning on buying another one soon, then ask the insurer if it's possible to keep the policy running till then (often called suspending cover) as this can be more cost effective.

You've got it sorted – well done!

Arranging car insurance for the first time is a major rite of passage. You can congratulate yourself for having got it over with – and cheer yourself up with the knowledge that now you've got your head round the system it'll be easier in the future.

Reference
Section

Driving organizations

For provisional and full licence enquiries

Driver and Vehicle Licensing Agency (DVLA)
Customer Enquiries (Drivers)
Swansea
SA6 7JL
Tel: 0870 240 0009
www.dvla.gov.uk

For test enquiries and bookings

Driving Standards Agency (DSA)
PO Box 280
Newcastle-upon-Tyne
NE99 1FP
Tel: 0870 0101 372
Welsh speakers: 0870 0100 372
www.dsa.gov.uk

Driving Standards Agency (Head Office)
Stanley House
56 Talbot St
Nottingham
NG1 5GU
Tel: 0115 901 2500
Email: customer.services@dsa.gsi.gov.uk

Driving Instructors Association
Safety House
Beddington Farm Road
Croydon
CRO 4XZ
Tel: 0208 665 5151
Local rate: 0845 345 5151
www.driving.org

For details of the Pass Plus course and a register of qualified instructors

Driving Standards Agency (DSA)
Pass Plus Unit
Stanley House
56 Talbot St
Nottingham
NG1 5GU
Tel: 0115 901 2633
www.passplus.org.uk

Disability contacts

The Forum of Mobility Centres
The national organization representing all mobility centres in the UK, which provides advice, information and driving assessments for disabled people.

c/o Providence Chapel
Warehorne
Ashford
Kent
TN26 2JX
Tel: 0800 559 3636
www.mobility-centres.org.uk

Queen Elizabeth's Foundation (QEF)
In addition to offering advice and assessments, QEF also runs courses for driving instructors on disability awareness and holds a countrywide register of instructors who have experience in teaching students with disabilities, including deaf students.

Mobility Centre
Damson Way
Fountain Drive
Carshalton
Surrey
SM5 4NR
Tel: 0208 770 1151
www.qef.org.uk/mobilitycentre

Online support groups for learner drivers

www.driving.org – The website of the Driving Instructors Association has a forum and chatroom. You can post questions about any driving-related issue and get advice from other students and instructors. It's also a good place to ask for recommendations for good local instructors.

www.2pass.co.uk – This site offers up-to-date information, an email newsletter and a busy learner driver forum.

www.handbag.com – This is a site aimed at women. Log on to the motoring forum on the discussion boards and swap tips with other girls.

Books and other resources on the technicalities of driving

Books

The Highway Code published by the Stationery Office (TSO). This contains the most up-to-date information on road safety and it's vital that its contents become hardwired into your brain.

Know Your Traffic Signs published by the Department for Transport. This contains most of the road signs and markings you are likely to come across.

The Official DSA Guide to Driving – The Essential Skills published by the DSA. Important advice on best driving practice.

The Official DSA Theory Test for Car Drivers (and The Highway Code) published by the Department for Transport. This book contains the entire bank of theory test questions, together with explanations for every answer. As it also contains the Highway Code it means you don't need to buy the two books. Absolutely essential reading.

Other study aids

The Official DSA Theory Test for Car Drivers (CD-ROM). This contains all the questions and answers and it also allows you to take mock tests using your home computer. Most learners who try out this approach find it really effective because it reproduces the test conditions.

You can take a mock test for the multiple choice part of the theory test online at www.dsa.gov.uk. The cost is approximately £6.99 for a thirty-day trial.

The Official DSA Guide to Hazard Perception (DVD). The DSA strongly recommends that you use this to prepare for the hazard perception part of the test. The DVD contains not only expert advice but also tips and quizzes. It also includes interactive hazard perception clips with feedback on your performance.

Focus Multimedia also produces theory test and hazard perception DVDs, together with a DVD on passing your practical test, featuring video tutorials of essential driving skills such as handling roundabouts and one-way streets and successfully completing the required manoeuvres. See www.focusmm.co.uk for more details.

Practice driving guides

Driving Standards Agency/Driver's Record approach: *Helping Learners to Practise – The Official DSA Guide.* The Driver's Record is based on the official learning to drive syllabus and lists all twenty-four key skills that you'll need to demonstrate to pass your test – such as reversing, correct use of speed, dealing with dual carriageways and so on. It can be downloaded free from www.dsa.gov.uk. The book also contains details of the record together with other tips for accompanying a learner.

Your driving instructor should be using a record like this in some form, and the skills are marked at different levels:

1. the skill is introduced
2. it can be carried out under full instruction
3. it can be carried out when prompted
4. it seldom needs to be prompted
5. you can carry it out consistently without any prompting

When you're at level 5 in all aspects of driving you're considered to be ready for your test. Obviously a formal approach like this is important for your driving lessons so that your instructor is able to follow your progress. However, having your nearest and dearest mark you for different skills can be a potentially volatile business. Only follow this approach if you're sure you're both able to handle it and that the learner won't end up pouting about how 'Rob only gave me a 3 for my bay park and I'm sure I deserved a 4.'

There is also the suggestion that your accompanying driver and instructor should discuss your progress. But if the prospect of your driving instructor and your partner or dad getting together and comparing notes on your inadequacies in the lane-discipline department, while you stand there hanging your head in shame, isn't particularly appealing, then you might want to pass on that. On the plus side, this approach does really focus you on your weak areas. And if you find you perform really well when out with your partner but consistently mess things up when you're with your instructor, then that would be worth analysing. It could be down to performance anxiety, which is something you'll need to work through. Alternatively it could be an indication that the dynamic between you and your instructor is one that makes you particularly tense and you'd be better off with someone else.

Supervising a Learner Driver published by the AA. The approach outlined here is considerably more relaxed and flexible. It's also one that can be adapted both for everyday driving and more structured practice sessions. Each chapter deals with different aspects of driving such as 'Use of Speed' or 'Starting on a Hill'. It gives advice on how to improve your skills in that area and also has a useful troubleshooting section for you and your companion to work out what might be going wrong and advice on how to correct it. And there's no marking system!

L

Coping with nerves

Hypnotherapy

National Council for Hypnotherapy
PO Box 421
Charwelton
Daventry
NN11 1AS
Tel: 0800 952 0545
www.hypnotherapists.org.uk

Hypnotherapy CD *Pass Your Driving Test* by Eddie Lester is available on Amazon and via www.hypnos.info.

Psychological approach

www.anxiousdriver.co.uk. This is a service run by psychologist Dr Joshua Carritt-Baker and his driving instructor father Colin Baker. It helps people with driving phobias and also has a list of driving instructors countrywide interested in working with anxious drivers.

16 The Charne
Otford
Nr Sevenoaks
Kent
TN14 5LS
Tel: 01959 524437

Buying a car

WhatCar magazine gives useful tips for buying new and used cars. It also has a useful website on www.whatcar.com. *Auto Trader* magazine offers used cars for sale. Their website at www.autotrader.co.uk gives advice for getting the best deal. www.parkers.co.uk is an informative used-car website which also has a useful forum where you can post questions about buying cars and car ownership in general.

Other useful organizations

Royal Society for the Prevention of Accidents (RoSPA)
RoSPA House
Edgbaston Park
353 Bristol Road
Edgbaston
Birmingham
B5 7ST
Tel: 0121 248 2000
www.rospa.com

RoSPA can also be contacted for details of the Experienced Driver Assessment.

The website has useful leaflets available for downloading, including *Helping Young People to Learn to Drive Safely*, *Parents and Young Drivers*, *Choosing Safer Vehicles* and *Safer Journey Planner*. RoSPA also runs the website www.helpingldrivers.com, which is dedicated to private practice for learner drivers.

The Suzy Lamplugh Trust
National Centre for Personal Safety
Hampton House
20 Albert Embankment
London
SE1 7TJ
Tel: 0207 091 0014
www.suzylamplugh.org.uk

This charity offers advice on safety to both women and men. They have useful advice on staying safe in your car available both on their website and in a variety of leaflets. They also run courses on personal safety.

Institute of Advanced Motorists (IAM)
IAM House
510 Chiswick High Road
London
W4 5RG
0208 996 9600
www.iam.org.uk

Kathy Higgins Dip. DI, driving consultant (Merseyside)
www.kathyhigginsdipdi.co.uk. Kathy is also a consultant trainer for Aigburth Driver Training at www.aigburthdriver training.co.uk.

Appendices

Appendix 1

Percentage pass rates by age and gender

Age	Female	Male
16	55.2	49.0
17	48.3	51.4
18	42.7	45.7
19	40.1	44.8
20	38.9	45.5
21	39.5	46.2
22	39.6	46.6
23	39.7	46.7
24	38.8	46.7
25	38.1	45.1
26	37.7	44.0
27	36.8	43.0
28	36.2	41.1
29	35.3	39.9
30	34.6	40.6
31	33.9	39.8
32	34.2	39.4
33	33.4	39.1
34	32.2	38.8

Age	Female	Male
35	31.4	38.6
36	31.9	39.0
37	30.1	37.8
38	30.7	37.3
39	30.5	37.1
40	29.1	37.7
41	27.9	36.9
42	28.7	37.9
43	28.2	35.4
44	27.4	37.9
45	26.0	35.6
46	27.9	37.4
47	25.1	35.3
48	26.9	34.6
49	24.1	34.5
50	25.4	32.2
51	25.3	36.7
52	26.9	35.8
53	25.8	38.2
54	25.6	37.1
55	27.5	35.6
56	22.2	37.8
57	27.4	37.5
58	24.4	40.1
59	26.0	30.5
60	27.2	31.0
61	24.7	38.4
62	21.7	29.7
63	24.5	40.9
64	19.9	36.7
65	20.4	35.3
66	17.0	35.9

Age	Female	Male
67	22.3	29.5
68	18.3	31.6
69	18.3	24.1
70	18.3	38.8
71	17.4	13.6
72	19.6	5.0
73	14.6	29.2
74	13.2	30.0
75	14.8	15.8
76	20.0	38.1
77	9.1	31.3
78	22.2	16.7
79	33.3	50.0
80	0.0	14.3
81	20.0	0.0
82	0.0	25.0
83	33.3	20.0
84	0.0	14.3
85	0.0	0.0
86	50.0	0.0
87	0.0	0.0
88	0.0	0.0
92	100.0	0.0

Figures from DSA Car Pass Rates by Age and Gender Survey 2004/5.

Appendix 2

Female pass rates by driving test centre

Does not include centres that have conducted less than 100 tests

London and South-East

Ashford (Kent)	46.0
Ashford (Middlesex)	44.6
Aylesbury	43.3
Banbury	50.9
Barking	29.5
Barnet	31.1
Belvedere	29.5
Bexleyheath	37.5
Bletchley	49.5
Borehamwood	33.0
Brighton	34.3
Broadstairs (Thanet)	41.4
Canterbury	41.6
Chertsey	46.1
Chichester	44.1
Crawley	39.1
Croydon	34.5

Eastbourne	43.3
Enfield	25.8
Folkestone	42.5
Gillingham L + LGV	37.4
Goodmayes	28.4
Gravesend	38.5
Greenford (Horsenden Lane)	29.1
Greenford (Ruislip Road)	40.0
Guildford L + LGV	42.8
Hastings	42.0
Hayes (Middlesex)	35.8
Hendon	35.7
Herne Bay	39.5
High Wycombe (Bucks)	45.6
Hither Green	34.0
Hornchurch	36.5
Hove	34.7
Isleworth	40.3
Maidstone	41.1
Mill Hill	32.3
Morden	46.3
Oxford (Cowley)	43.6
Pinner	42.0
Reigate	42.4
Sevenoaks	41.1
Sidcup	37.6
Southall	38.4
South Norwood	31.1
Sutton (Surrey)	40.0
Tolworth	42.7
Tunbridge Wells	46.3
Wallington (Mint House)	37.9
Wanstead	30.9

Wanstead (Nightingale Lane)	31.3
West Wickham (Kent)	41.0
Weybridge	47.5
Winchmore Hill	31.0
Wood Green	26.5
Worthing	40.9

Midlands and Eastern

Bedford	42.5
Birmingham (Kings Heath)	29.5
Birmingham (Kingstanding)	36.3
Birmingham (Quinton)	27.1
Birmingham (Shirley)	43.7
Birmingham (South Yardley)	36.7
Birmingham (Sutton Coldfield)	41.1
Birmingham (Washwood Heath)	36.0
Bishops Stortford	42.6
Boston	47.4
Brentwood	28.8
Burton-on-Trent	39.4
Bury St Edmunds, Suffolk	37.7
Buxton	41.3
Cambridge (Chesterton Road)	49.7
Cambridge (Cowley Road)	47.3
Cannock	42.3
Chelmsford	31.3
Chesterfield	31.2
Chingford	31.1
Clacton-on-Sea	37.0
Colchester	34.2
Coventry (Bayton Road)	34.4
Derby (Sinfin Lane)	40.5
Gainsborough	43.1

Grantham	47.5
Grays	31.2
Hereford	44.6
Hinckley	50.0
Ipswich	40.3
Kettering	41.3
Kidderminster	44.8
Kings Lynn	49.6
Leicester (Gipsy Lane)	32.3
Leicester (Welford Road)	32.4
Leicester (Wigston)	38.1
Leighton Buzzard	45.9
Letchworth	39.8
Lichfield	45.7
Lincoln	40.9
Loughborough	39.7
Loughton	31.2
Louth	45.4
Lower Gornal	41.3
Lowestoft	43.2
Ludlow	52.4
Luton	38.2
Melton Mowbray	42.0
Newcastle-under-Lyme	36.0
Northampton	39.5
Norwich (Midlands Jupiter Road)	43.4
Nottingham (Chalfont Drive)	33.3
Nottingham (Gedling)	37.7
Nottingham (West Bridgford)	39.0
Nuneaton	44.6
Oswestry	50.1
Peterborough	44.5
Redditch (Worcestershire)	39.1

Rugby	46.6
St Albans	42.8
Shrewsbury	45.4
Skegness	43.4
Southend-On-Sea	32.8
Spalding	44.4
Stafford	41.9
Stevenage	40.6
Stoke-on-Trent (Cobridge)	41.1
Sutton-in-Ashfield (Midlands)	41.0
Telford	47.8
Warwick	42.7
Watford	41.5
Wednesbury	32.5
Wellingborough	42.9
Whitchurch	49.4
Wisbech	45.6
Wolverhampton	40.6
Worcester	39.5
Worksop	36.5

Northern

Alnwick	48.1
Barnsley	30.1
Barrow-in-Furness	45.2
Berwick-upon-Tweed	46.8
Bishop Auckland	38.1
Blackburn	37.1
Blackpool	38.9
Blyth	38.2
Bolton	42.1
Bradford	30.6
Bradford (Heaton)	25.8

Bridlington	41.2
Bury, Lancs.	40.3
Carlisle	36.6
Cheetham Hill – Manchester	45.2
Chester	38.0
Chorley	41.6
Cleethorpes	38.3
Congleton	44.5
Crewe	46.6
Darlington	40.4
Doncaster	44.7
Durham	41.3
Ellesmere Port	45.9
Failsworth	41.7
Garston	42.7
Gateshead	34.0
Halifax	38.2
Harrogate	42.5
Hartlepool	36.5
Heckmondwike	26.8
Hessle	38.3
Hexham	36.3
Heysham	44.4
Horsforth	34.1
Huddersfield	31.4
Hull	41.6
Hyde	36.2
Keighley	42.8
Kendal	46.3
Kenton Bar	33.2
Leeds (Harehills)	25.9
Longbenton	33.0
Macclesfield	44.8

Malton	51.0
Middlesbrough	38.5
Nelson	35.4
Norris Green	42.4
Northallerton	46.8
Northwich (Northern)	44.9
Pontefract	39.3
Preston	43.1
Reddish (Northern)	44.7
Rochdale	39.2
Rotherham	32.4
St Helens	40.7
Sale	41.4
Scarborough	42.2
Scunthorpe	41.6
Sheffield (Handsworth)	37.8
Sheffield (Middlewood Road)	40.9
Skipton	42.6
Southport	45.3
South Shields	39.1
Sunderland	34.1
Thornaby	40.1
Upton	43.2
Wakefield	27.4
Wallasey	37.5
Warrington	42.2
Whalley Range – Manchester	39.5
Whitby	49.3
Wigan	45.6
Widnes	39.4
York	44.1

Scotland

Aberdeen (Altens)	47.7
Aberdeen (Balgownie Road)	40.9
Aberfeldy	60.0
Airdrie	32.8
Alness	46.4
Arbroath	47.7
Ayr	41.6
Ballachulish	50.0
Ballater	63.7
Banff	50.8
Barra Island	56.3
Bathgate	44.2
Benbecula Island	40.6
Blairgowrie	55.1
Brodick (Isle of Arran)	73.9
Buckie	50.9
Callander	39.6
Campbeltown	57.5
Castle Douglas	53.4
Crieff	51.1
Cumnock	52.0
Cupar	54.9
Dumbarton	40.0
Dumfries	43.7
Dundee	40.7
Dunfermline	44.5
Dunoon	57.4
Duns	56.2
Edinburgh (Currie)	43.7
Edinburgh (Joppa)	42.9
Falkirk	39.4
Forfar	54.2

Fort William	45.7
Fraserburgh	39.7
Gairloch	59.3
Galashiels	52.5
Girvan	51.8
Glasgow (Anniesland)	35.6
Glasgow (Baillieston)	31.5
Glasgow (Mosspark)	28.2
Glasgow (Springburn Park)	38.1
Golspie	38.7
Grantown-on-Spey	57.8
Greenock	40.6
Haddington	51.7
Hamilton	36.1
Hawick	44.9
Huntly	57.8
Inveraray (Argyll)	54.3
Inverness	43.0
Inverurie (Grampian)	48.9
Islay Island	45.9
Island of Mull (Salen)	37.5
Isle of Skye (Broadford)	59.0
Isle of Skye (Portree)	49.3
Isle of Tiree	75.0
Kelso	48.9
Kilmarnock	39.0
Kingussie	65.0
Kyle of Lochalsh	48.8
Lairg	57.9
Lanark	44.7
Lerwick (Shetland)	62.4
Lochgilphead	57.5
Mallaig	60.0

Montrose	54.3
Newton Stewart	54.5
Oban	46.4
Orkney (Kirkwall)	48.0
Paisley	39.4
Peebles	47.7
Perth	38.7
Peterhead	41.2
Pitlochry	64.7
Rothesay (Bute Island)	51.7
Saltcoats	43.4
South Uist Island	36.4
Stirling	36.1
Stonehaven	48.5
Stornoway (Lewis)	48.6
Stranraer	52.6
Thurso	44.2
Ullapool	34.0
Wick	45.9
Wishaw	38.7

Wales and Western

Abergavenny	46.8
Aberystwyth (Park Avenue)	50.9
Aldershot	43.5
Bala	39.2
Bangor	45.3
Barnstaple	44.8
Barry	41.2
Basingstoke	42.4
Bodmin	46.8
Bournemouth	45.9
Brecon	47.9

Bridgend	43.3
Bristol (Brislington)	39.9
Bristol (St George)	43.4
Bristol (Southmead)	42.1
Camborne L + LGV	48.8
Cardiff (Fairwater)	44.1
Cardigan	48.1
Carmarthen	50.9
Cheltenham	44.6
Chippenham	49.2
Colwyn Bay	34.4
Cwmbran	43.8
Dorchester	49.8
Exeter	42.5
Gloucester	45.2
Gosport	42.1
Haverfordwest L + LGV	43.4
Holyhead	48.6
Isles of Scilly	50.0
Lampeter	50.9
Launceston	46.3
Llandrindod Wells	54.1
Llanelli	44.2
Merthyr Tydfil	45.6
Minehead	52.1
Mold	39.1
Monmouth	47.8
Newbury	40.9
Newport (Isle of Wight)	47.8
Newton Abbot	45.0
Newtown	49.0
Pembroke Dock	42.9
Penzance	43.0

Plymouth	37.8
Pontypridd	47.8
Portsmouth	42.3
Pwllheli	52.6
Reading	39.7
Rhyl	30.1
Salisbury	46.0
Slough	41.5
Southampton (Forest Hills)	40.6
Southampton (Maybush)	45.3
Swansea	44.3
Swindon	41.3
Taunton	49.2
Trowbridge	48.4
Weston-super-Mare	46.2
Winchester	42.9
Wrexham	37.1
Yeovil	49.2

Figures are for 1 April 2005 to 31 March 2006 from DSA.

Index